LIFE HAS NO MEANING UNTIL YOU CREATE IT

By Rinus Le Roux

COPYRIGHT AND PUBLISHING

CONTENTS

OTHER PUBLICATIONS BY THE SAME AUTHOR

- Personal Greatness – 2003
- Missing Pages from Life's Manual – 2004
- From Successful to Meaningful – 2007
- Step Up – 2008
- We will be OK – 2009
- Passport to the Future – 2011

DEDICATION

This book is dedicated to Hendrik Heystek who showed me that in the absence of ego, the spirit grows. R.I.P.

INVITE RINUS

You can invite me to speak at your next function, meeting or conference.

Go to **www.ucan.co.za** and follow me on facebook or twitter.

Email me on **rinus@ucan.co.za**

ACKNOWLEDGEMENTS

This may be the page that the reader skips over to get to the content but, to the author, this may be the most important page as it is here where I thank, from the bottom of my heart, the following:

- The Muse who with this book has been especially kind and gentle. Her voice was soft but firm. Wherever you are, I hope to feel you again soon.
- Hanlie for deciphering my handwriting and for correcting all those spelling mysteries while typing my books. I love you.
- The friends and colleagues who endorsed the book. It was kind of you to link your names to my book.
- Lisa who is always willing to think about my brand and how to style it.
- Valda for questioning me and coming up with wonderful ways to streamline my words.
- Angus, you mean more to me than my banker. I always appreciate your sharpening the pencil.
- Merwelene for having the creativity to see my best angle through your lens.
- Danie for making the stunning marks on the canvas.
- My friends, family, business partners and all my clients who allow me to interact with them in a meaningful way.
- You the reader. I am because of you.

ENDORSEMENTS FOR THE BOOK

'Rinus is a genius! He is right ... "Life has no Meaning... until you create it". This new 'blockbuster' is a must read whether it is for your personal life or your career advancement. Once again I'll be giving away another book by Rinus to my friends and clients. Rinus is right up there with the best international authors in the world. Read it, use it and live it ... and receive the unlimited benefits of creating the right meaning for you in your life.'

Bill Gibson (Author of Boost Your Business in Any Economy, International speaker/sales specialist/entrepreneur and Chairperson of Knowledge Brokers International)

'Rinus epitomises a person who lives a meaningful life as described in this, his latest book – and he does it with great passion and enthusiasm!'

Brand Pretorius (Director of Companies)

To Rinus, 'In life, you must paint a picture which is appreciated by others in order to be of satisfaction to yourself.'

Clem Sunter (Scenario Planner)

'In SARS we endeavour to create an institution where individuals provide a significant service and experience themselves as playing

meaningful roles for good. Rinus' interaction with SARS focused on shaping such behaviours of individuals.'

Ivan Pillay (Deputy Commissioner – SARS)

'Rinus is a free thinker and in a changing world that is what we all need to be. This book holds the potential for you to have a more meaningful life.'

Jenna Clifford (Art Jeweller/entrepreneur/philanthropist)

'Rinus le Roux has, for the last ten years, been exhorting the readers of The Star Workplace, through his fortnightly columns, to make meaning of their lives, and assuring them that they can do it. 'In the process he has committed his extended thinking to paper via six books. This is his seventh, continues down that road. Those who read it will receive the tools to go out and create a life that is more than mere existence.'

Theo Garrun (Editor - The Star Workplace)

'Rinus has discovered the art of executing a meaningful life. His work on "meaning" is pivotal, bold and should be required reading for those who know there is more to success.'

Timothy Maurice Webster (Author – Personivation)

'Self-doubt, anxiety and fear are debilitating to many people in the world today. The world needs hope, inspiration, empowerment and the ability to make meaning. In creating meaning, each one of us has the

power to reset the stage of life by making the choices we believe in. We can choose to rewrite the script, or change the characters, the geography, the decor ... even when you are astonished by the challenges life might toss you, you can make meaning.'

Prof. Shirley Zinn (Human Resources Director of Standard Bank South Africa and the Deputy Global Head of Human Resources for the Standard Bank Group)

INTRODUCTION

Have you ever discovered or created something so special and so unique – possibly an idea, a saying, a thought, a plan, a new way of doing something – that you are almost afraid to try to translate it into reality?

Is the reason for your fear the fact that once you do so, this 'thing' will have to be subjected to the judgement, criticism and opinions of other people? Do you sometimes feel so insecure about exposing this pet concept of yours to the test of scrutiny in the real world that you think it safer to keep it in your head and heart?

Well, that is the case with this book. Such a lot happened during the time leading up to my writing these words with my black pen in my moleskin notepad ...

I have spent many years teaching a program called 'The Meta-Meaning Program'. I also made a CD called 'The Meaning Maker' and have written countless newspaper and magazine articles on how to create meaning. I have engaged with numerous companies where I did one-to-one and group sessions with staff members on meaning in one's personal and work life.

Ironically, I had completed about sixty percent of the book when I lost all my material – needless to say I was devastated.

The frustration I felt over not being able to give birth to this book, so that it could leave my head and my soul to find its rightful place and stand its ground in the real world, meant that for months I didn't attempt to even rewrite the chapter headings or recreate the layout.

The turning point eventually came through the one-to-one interviews I mentioned earlier. A number of these touched my being very deeply. Through them I learned such a lot and the information in my head very slowly, like honey, began to trickle from my heart to my hand and the concepts, text and layout all started to cohere and flow once again. So you are now reading the result of the most tedious writing process I've ever had to endure. Soon you will be able to form an opinion about what I have written and make a call as to whether or not you think my ideas are useful to you. The truth is that itreally doesn't matter.

I hope that by reading these pages you will learn that meaning isn't something that exists 'out there'. The potential to create it exists within you and only you can do so. Although a number of factors contribute to your experience of meaning, it cannot exist without you as modifier.

My wish remains that this book will add value to your life, but I've come to realise that my writing is a personal experience and I cannot do it or not do it for the sake of anyone else. The same is true of your life. Your life is about your experience of meaning, and you cannot not be you or be a fake you for someone else. Meaning either exists or doesn't exist because of you. You are its creator.

In the beginning,
as they said, there
was nothing, and
nothing could exist
because of the absence
of something. At the
instant of creation of
something, whatever
it may be, nothing
ceases to exist.

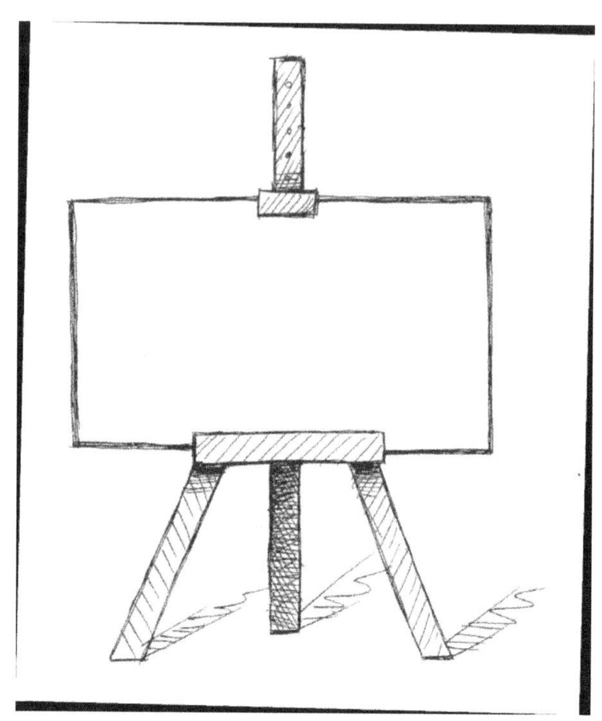

LIFE HAS NO MEANING

'Life is a blank canvas. You are as responsible for the markings on your canvas as I am for the markings on mine.'

Life has no meaning

Most thinking human adults have, from time to time, paused to ask themselves this question: 'What is the meaning of life?' You have probably done so yourself although you may have phrased the question slightly differently. In one way or another we all, at some point, come to ask this question even though we don't really expect to be able to answer it. In posing this perplexing question, we join the fraternity of thinkers who wonder what 'it' all means.

Joining this fraternity wouldn't be necessary if someone had come up with a solid answer by now. Had that been the case, we'd have no need to throw up our hands in the air because the answer would have been taught in our schools, universities, places of worship and in the homes in which we grew up.

You need only take note of the number of books in the self-help or psychology sections of a bookstore to understand that there is an overwhelming need to find answers to all the big questions of life. Even the philosophical vagueness of many of the titles indicates the elusiveness of these answers –

Man's Search for Meaning, The Secret, In Search of Excellence, Conversations with God – not to mention the vast range of0 'how to' books, and books on religion and the spiritual teachings of the world. If one takes an overview of all these, the conclusion may well be reached that there is no meaning, no certainty and no correct answer. Everyone is trying to find

their own truth and their own reality.

Let's then agree, for now, that life has no meaning, or at least admit that no one knows exactly what the meaning of life is.

The blank canvas

The embryo is formed and approximately forty weeks later a mother gives birth to a new body, a new mind and a new soul – in many ways a blank canvas. From now on, every day will etch the markings of experience on this canvas. Conditioning, values, principles, skills and all the other elements we are exposed to in the course of living will shape not only the detailed image but also the landscape and background of the painting. This canvas will, for the rest of its time here, accumulate more markings day by day, some more deeply ingrained in memory than others.

If you can agree with this and perhaps, for a while, ignore such factors as instinct, DNA and reincarnation, we can begin to think about how meaning is created on a subjective level on a blank canvas where there is no meaning to begin with.

The metaphor of the canvas is slightly paradoxical as we know that any mark made on it has an effect on our lives, but we also know that we can paint over it, erase it, bleach it and colour it differently. Modern psychology has shown that markings can be erased from the conscious mind to the extent that they will have little or no effect on our future lives.

However, the fact remains that the marks have been made and, whether we erase them or paint over them, doesn't alter this fact. Perhaps the ancient sages knew this to be true and therefore stressed the importance of the quality of every thought and every experience as these leave indelible marks on the psyche.

Stroke of Meaningfulness

In a karate tournament final, I once faced a formidable opponent who had the reputation of giving no respect to any of his opponents. As we faced each other, moments before we assumed the fighting position, a friend standing near me said, 'This is your moment. Nothing that happened in the past counts for anything. Make this moment count!' The canvas is yours – make it count.

Uncertainty and limitless possibilities

Among my circle of friends and acquaintances, and in my culture, I have not met many people who thrive on uncertainty.

In fact, most people I know will go to great lengths to eliminate uncertainties and convert them to certainties. Even our language has stigmatised uncertainty with statements and questions such as:

- I am in the dark.
- What are my options?
- I wish I knew.
- Do you have word on ...?
- Have you heard yet?
- Give me the scenarios, etc, etc.

All of these strive to eliminate or minimise uncertainty and narrow down the possibilities to a few, or more ideally, just one single uncertainty. In some way, we tend to feel that we can deal better with one solid fact, whether it is positive or negative, than with a vast array of possibilities.

The only problem with certainty is that it limits your options. If you have certainty all options are eliminated. Imagine having the ability to deal with uncertainty while simultaneously

keeping all of your options open – to maintain the blank canvas that allows all the great artists to pour out ideas on what markings could be made on it. Suddenly there is unlimited potential. The more alternatives you have, the better your chances of creating meaning and significance.

To create more meaning we will have to embrace that blank canvas and become more comfortable with uncertainty.

This will give rise to more options and to have more options to choose from will give us more possibilities. These possibilities are what we need to create greater fulfilment and growth.

A few years ago a good friend of mine had to buy his own business back from a financial institution. This was necessary in order to protect his intellectual property. During this

painstaking process of negotiation he unexpectedly ran into cash-flow problems. He had an agreement with the financial

institution that owned the majority share in the company to share all income derived from his products and training.

This arrangement just didn't work out and he almost became financially crippled.

In the midst of all of this he was diagnosed with melanoma on his leg, which had to be removed, with a number of medical tests to follow. His family and friends obviously hoped and

prayed that it wasn't cancer and that he would be fine. We all wanted the certainty that he was fine, but the melanoma turned out to be cancerous. Fortunately, post surgery, he was given a clean bill of health.

Here comes the interesting part: Amidst all the tests my friend underwent to determine that he had cancer, the uncertainty of his future, the possibility of having to undergo chemotherapy and not knowing how his body would respond to it, his broker mentioned to him that one of his insurance policies covered him for dread disease. A claim was submitted and he was paid out just over a million rand. This freed him up to buy back his business, solve his cash-flow problems and get back on his feet to run his very useful and successful business. In this case, uncertainty gave rise to a number of possibilities that culminated in a very positive outcome for him. This health-scare occurred a few years ago and his health – both physical and financial – is now in great shape.

When starting out with a blank canvas, one has no idea how the painting one will create will eventually turn out, but before you apply the first brushstrokes the possibilities are limitless.

Get comfortable with uncertainty.

THE ABILITY TO CREATE

'Every thought, every word and every deed carries
the latent potential to create a better world.'

Every single one of us has the ability to create. We create thoughts, words, situations, stories, feelings, art, music, buildings and, yes, we even procreate. So when someone says he or she is not creative, what they usually mean is that they lack the ability to express their creativity in an artistic way. This does not mean they cannot and do not create. We all create all the time.

Planet earth's polar opposites provide us with endless options. If something is not light it is dark, not near then far, not beautiful then ugly, and not good then bad – and all the myriad permutations of these absolutes. Thus we have a choice in what we are going to create – the good, the beautiful, the useful, the positive or the opposites thereof.

This then brings us to the most important consequence of creation which is responsibility. We have to take responsibility for the thoughts, words and deeds we create. Whether you are an artist creating a painting or you create thoughts in your mind, there has to be a level of responsibility that accompanies this process. This responsibility is towards the self and towards all that is external to the self.

A concept that the post-modern individual has become comfortable with is that we co create our lives. This implies that, together with the creator or a force of creation, we partake in giving gestalt to our lives. We are not at the mercy of the creator or a force of creation, but rather partners in creation. Through free will we make choices and through these choices we influence the quality and the outcome of our lives here on earth. As much as it is wonderful to know we have that power, it is also frightening because we then become co-responsible for everything that happens to us on the planet. On the basis of this premise, we are not only responsible for our own lives but we co-create a world where other people are affected by our thoughts, words and deeds and how we execute our choices.

Now that we know we have the infinite ability to create, it's fascinating to discover that there is a limitless source of inspiration, almost like a fountain that pours from it all things – art, poetry, sculpture, music, books, computer

applications, information and so much more. It's so exciting to know that you and I are part of this creative process and that as cocreators we get to participate in it.

One of the most amazing aspects of this process of creation is that shifts take place when groups of people, communities, governments and so on put their belief behind projects and change what needs to be changed in the world. For example, if saving the whales receives enough 'positive' support from not only those who try and save the whales, but also from you and I, the possibility of protecting this endangered species against extinction increases exponentially, all because of higher levels of consciousness. For scientists to find cures for cancer and AIDS they need a mindset of possibility, but they also need belief and support from you and I. Our power to co-create lies far deeper than we realise. We literally control the consciousness of this planet and the future of everything that was, is and ever will be.

During my own process of writing, speaking and creating programs, I discovered a great truth which is that when you are busy creating, you should be mindful that your primary role is that of conduit, messenger, giver that allows the greater good to manifest through you. Herein lies the fulfilment in creating.

If we focus on our ability to co-create, we can bring peace to the world, solve poverty and live meaningful lives. We can do all this and so much more by pooling our creative powers.

THE MASKS OF MEANING

'Behind every mask hides personal truth, waiting to reveal its authenticity.'

THE MASKS OF MEANING

The greatest barrier that stands between us and a meaningful life must undoubtedly be the ego. As our consciousness develops and evolves, so does the cunning of the ego. It takes on a number of faces, all of which masquerade as significance, whereas in actual fact it impedes us in our quest for true, meaningful and authentic experience.

In this chapter you will discover the various masks of meaning held up by the unauthentic self. We have all worn some of these masks in order to feel more meaningful, only to discover that all we experienced was a short-lived illusion of self-importance which does not equate with true significance.

These masks are:

I am what I do

The one question you can be sure to be asked at any work related or social gathering is 'What do you do?' Whether merely out of habit or real interest on the part of person asking this question, we all attach a lot of value to what people do for a living. Not that this indicates a problem or a sign of shallowness. This only becomes a problem when we define ourselves by what we do, when it determines the sum total of who we are. You too have probably had the unfortunate experience of having to listen ad infinitum and ad nauseam to individuals who can only talk about what they do, what their jobs and responsibilities are, and how important these are.

They (perhaps we) tend to go on for hours while demonstrating our significance by explaining to others what we do and how we do it.

At a recent social gathering I found myself in conversation with a secondary school teacher. At first we hit it off, talking about education and its importance. However, two hours later we had still not moved on to finding solutions for education, discussing our personal education or even education in the first and third worlds. We were still stuck on the details of her life story as a teacher. The weirdest part was that, judging by how much she complained, one would have thought she would be happy to change the topic or even explore some opportunities to improve education. The realisation that she was unable to define herself as anything other than a disgruntled teacher came when I eventually succeeded in mingling with other people at the gathering only to overhear her having exactly the same non-constructive conversation with another victim.

What we do can easily consume us and become the only thing that provides us with meaning. As we will see later on, making a contribution and adding value is of paramount importance in creating meaning, but if your perceived value equals only what you do, you are wearing this mask. Perhaps part of the problem originates in our early conditioning. As a child you arrive home from school and the first question your parents ask is 'What did you do today?'

Later on, you get home after a day's work and the person you live with asks 'What did you do today?' In this way we learn that our value is determined by what we do rather than by who we are. At my ten-year school reunion, the majority of the conversation was devoted to establishing what each one of us had done with our lives career-wise since leaving school. Some even went so far as to hire a special car for the day in order to demonstrate that their success at what they were doing for a living also gave them the means to afford a flashy and expensive car! (Wonderful to see how all of that had changed by the time our 30-year reunion rolled around.)

Those who had gone on to study and had become qualified professionals or had achieved material success in some other area of endeavour were definitely more arrogant than those who had not enjoyed the same opportunities or 'breaks'. The bulk of the conversation, as mentioned, revolved around our efforts to demonstrate the significance we'd achieved though our careers.

It was Neale Donald Walsch who once said that we should not forget that we are not human doings, but human beings.

Herein lies the key to our existence and the means of debunking the fallacy that we create meaning through the job title or position we hold, even the size of the office we occupy, how many people we have reporting to us, the budgets we manage, the power we have to allow underlings to advance or not, or any other self-important thing we may do.

In essence you are so much more than what you do. It is important to discover this truth long before you retire or become either mentally or physically incapable of carrying out the functions of the job you are employed to do. If you leave it that late, your whole experience of value will be warped and you might live with debilitating discontent for the rest of your life. Whereas, if you know that your value lies beyond your working years, beyond the title you hold and even beyond the charity you support, you will be able to create meaning for yourself until the day you exhale for the last time.

I am my reputation

'Do you know who I am ...?' We have all heard this egotistical statement meaning 'My reputation is common knowledge.

Unless you are mentally deficient or not connected to the "right" people my name should be familiar to you and you should know of me and what I can do.'

So many celebrities and well-known people wear this particular mask – they live by their reputation. They are careful not to be seen with the wrong people at the wrong places and at the wrong times because they are their reputations and nothing more. This mask is painted with war paint and patched with extraordinary achievements. They display their awards on the mantelpiece and their framed certificates on the wall.

However it is not only celebrities and well-known people who wear this mask but rather ordinary people like you and I who received recognition at some stage in life and have hung our egos on those achievements to the extent that we keep trotting them out at every available opportunity regardless of whether they are still relevant. The same reunion I mentioned earlier was attended by the school's fastest athlete and star sportsman. He didn't go to university and had become a bit of a drifter. You can probably imagine how his attempts to brag revolved solely around his sporting achievements while still a teenager at school. They all started with 'Do you remember when I ...'

There is no doubt that a good reputation serves you well, but it should not be the only criterion that determines your value.

Living in the past rapes the value of the present. The objective is to experience yourself as significant and valuable in all phases of your life. Later in this book you will see that it is possible to find personal value and meaning without having to cling to some achievement in your past or bank on your past reputation to get you through the present moment. You have the opportunity to create meaning in every moment.

Reputation, like all other masks, is an illusion; it is a crutch from the past that has no true value in the present. Your reputation as a reference point is good to have, but your value lies in the value you can create here and now in the present. The truth is that if you have faith in yourself and your authenticity, it is far better to enjoy the value you create in the present than to rely solely on and reminisce about the accolades of the past.

I am what I have

I am my family, I am my job, I am my house, I am my religion, I am my intellect, I am my ability to ..., I am my body, I am my money ...

This may well be the mask we most struggle to remove. It is so easy to derive value and meaning from what we have because it is so tangible, so measurable and so easy to compare with those who have more, the same or less.

When Cain killed Abel, it was because Abel made a fire the smoke from which went straight up and Cain's didn't. Abel had something Cain didn't. Since the beginning of time we see how people measure personal value and significance in terms of what they have. In biblical terms it was said that it would be easier for a camel to go through the eye of a needle than it would be for a rich man to enter the kingdom of heaven. This has nothing to do with being materially rich but rather that, if you identify your value with what you own and have, you cannot receive the true blessings of life, including the reward of 'going to heaven'.

The paradox is that we think we own stuff but the truth is that the stuff owns us. For example, when the diamond ring that has been in the family for many generations gets lost, it is almost as if the whole family loses its significance – not to mention the family farm, the custom of studying medicine or law, etc, etc. Individuals, families, communities and countries build their value on what they have. The problem with anything that you can own is that it is of temporary value.

Diamonds, land, intellect, skills, etc merely constitute 'stuff' that gives temporary value which can and will be lost in the fullness of time.

So, when you choose to attach value to what you have, know that, given enough time, you will lose it and, if your value is perceived as an inextricable part of what you own, you will lose that too.

This most definitely doesn't mean you shouldn't own anything.

It merely means that you shouldn't become so attached to your material possessions that what you own starts owning you to the extent that 'its' value becomes your value and its appreciation equates to the stroking of your ego needs to tell you that you are okay and valuable.

John Lennon, in the song 'Imagine', said: *'Imagine no country.*

It's easy if you try, and then imagine no possessions. I wonder if you can?' He asks this question because it's really so difficult to distance ourselves from our possessions when they possess us rather than the other way around.

The Buddhist endeavours to live a life of non-attachment because once there is attachment, there is discontent. As we know, the only constant in life is change and that which we are attached to will change. Yet we are reluctant to let go of the past and our hankering after attachments connected with that past can be the source of great unhappiness.

Perhaps the lesson to learn is that although you may own materially valuable things, the one thing that is sure is that your value lies far beyond the things you own.

Looking back on my own life I will have to plead guilty of wearing all three of the masks of meaning at various times and, make no mistake, at the time I was unaware of hiding

behind them. I thought the masks I was wearing reflected the real me. Through being mindful of your own consciousness you will become more aware of how these masks present themselves.

In conclusion it is absolutely fine to have a reputation, to desire material things and to love what you do. In fact, that is life as we know it. The masks only take on a negative significance if they become your crutches, meaning that you use them as a yardstick against which to measure how meaningful your life is. There is no problem with the following statement: 'I am doing well. I am a contributor to my family, my company

and my country. I have worked hard to own what I own and I have a good reputation.' The problem only comes in when you define yourself as no more and no less than that. In truth you are so much more than that and, if you are not going to explore your potential beyond what you own and what you have achieved so far, you are selling yourself short.

A Stroke of Meaningfulness

When I reflect back on my life it is easy to identify the masks I wore, the insecurities I had to struggle with. Sometimes it is just easier to wear the mask than to face the truth and be yourself. There was a time I was my hair, my motorcycle, my car and the girlfriend on my arm. I excelled in sport and my reputation was another mask I wore only to find out that all of these things can be taken away, even the hair on my head.

BECOME THE MEANING MAKER

'When you hear the call and respond with YES, you are transforming into the Meaning Maker.'

According to popular psychology, we know that if you can name something you can claim it, the concept being that the mind allows us to move forward much more easily and more quickly if there is a complete and encapsulated idea. It works the same way with mental issues, physical issues and emotional issues – hence the idea to name those who choose to have and create meaning in their lives as Meaning Makers. In the pages that follow you will find that meaning doesn't just magically appear on the blank canvas; it takes on gestalt when we create it.

The term 'Meaning Maker' represents all of us who actively pursue a lifelong journey to fill our lives with significance and meaning. On this journey you may find the following beacons to light your way.

Possibility thinking

As a characteristic this could be the most important trait for the Meaning Maker to have. As a mindset, possibility thinking postulates that everything is possible. Possibility is not confined to what we sense as possible; thinking that something is impossible doesn't make it impossible. For instance, creating a vaccine against polio, air travel, space exploration and so forth were all at some point considered 'impossible' to achieve. The people who made these things happen didn't share that mindset of impossibility. To the contrary, they held exactly the opposite mindset.

An empowering tool for the Meaning Maker is to hold the mindset of possibility. One can admit that one cannot see how a particular thing is possible, but still be humble enough to say that it is only one's own view and one is not so arrogant as to think that this view dictates what is possible or not.

I again learned this lesson in a fun way while doing my military service. Always hungry as a 'soldier', a friend asked me if I felt like eating French fries. I laughed and said yes, but where would we find this rare treat at 21h00 in a military camp? He suggested that we could buy some from a machine – which I took to be a joke. However, when we walked to the cafeteria, lo and behold, outside was a vending machine that dispensed hot French fries! Needless to say I lost the bet I had made with my friend that such a thing was impossible.

The best we can do for ourselves and our world is to adopt the mindset that everything is possible even if we cannot envisage it at the time.

A new reality

Although the world has woken up to the fact that reality is relative, many people still believe it is static and that whatever is real is real. I like Einstein's little story about gravity and relativity. He disagreed with Newton who claimed that if an apple falls from a tree, the reality is that it will hit the ground.

Einstein retorted that this is not a reality; it is only relatively true because he could sit under the tree and catch the apple before it hits the ground.

The aim here is to dispel the 'truth' that reality is real to everyone in the same way. The 'truth' is that reality is relative and is a condition of the observer's perception, hence the term 'perceptive reality'. Yes, we create our own reality. In the world of the Meaning Maker this is very significant because if you can shift your perception of something you can also shift your reality and give birth to a new reality.

Through group consciousness we create certain perceptions, build them into our language and cement them into our belief system. These then become our reality. For instance, we all refer to a sunrise and a sunset, whereas we all know that the sun is stationary and the earth revolves around it which gives rise to the illusion of a sunrise and a sunset. There are many more examples of things we believe to be part of a fixed reality but, on closer inspection, we find that they are very far from real. The only reality is the perception and these perceptions can be changed.

Knowing this becomes a very powerful tool when we challenge ourselves to create meaning and dispel old realities that might be hampering us on our journey.

The power of choice

Yes, you can stay on the couch and do no harm because you do nothing – that is your choice. Or you can choose to activate the dormant faculties in your brain, come alive with energy and begin the journey towards meaning. This is the promise of the power of choice. We choose the thoughts we have, the words we speak and the deeds we do.

Psychologists have often stated that between the stimulus and response there is a gap and in that gap we choose how we are going to respond. This, according to psychologists, is where our power lies; we can control the outcome by choosing a better response.

Whether you believe that we have free will or not, one must admit that the ability to choose, whether the choice emanates from our genetic pre-disposition or is a function of free will, gives us power over our destiny and over the quality of our

future.

With the power of choice comes responsibility. Choosing is the easy part, but following through and taking responsibility for your choice is more difficult. For example, one might wake up one morning and choose to have a brilliant day. Minutes later, however, things start going sideways and it's all too easy to lose sight of this choice. It is here that responsibility for your choice and your free will come in. Now you have to honour that choice.

The power of choice has a tremendous impact on our lives and the world we live in. It literally means that we can right now choose, individually and collectively, to live in a better and more peaceful world. Isn't it wonderful to know that the power to achieve this ideal lies within us?

The journey

Joseph Campbell wrote about the Hero's Journey and how we all, at some stage in our lives, hear the call to live our purpose, to make a difference and to become the Meaning Maker. He then plotted a complete journey of the Hero (or rather you and I) who responds to the call. This journey has many aspects and takes us through many trials and tribulations, back to the point where we as individuals return with something of value – a truth, an understanding, a virtue, a principle or a story of significance – to take back and share with our tribe so that their lives can become more meaningful. This journey of the Hero is the journey of the Meaning Maker, the one who chooses to react to the call and embark on the journey.

At the age of thirteen, I heard the call – a soft whisper, almost too soft, more like a passive suggestion from somewhere. I tried to respond but had no idea what this call was all about.

When the call became louder and more insistent, it made me feel uneasy, as if I should know what to do, where to get the information I needed and how to respond. Still, I did not feel that I was making any headway until all I did was say 'YES' to indicate in some very subtle way that I wanted to take the journey. This was literally all the universe was waiting for. From nowhere and everywhere I began to connect with people, information, mentors, examples, indicators and

Meaning Makers. The essence of it all is that when you say 'YES', give a nod of the head, affirm your commitment in the soul, a positive activation takes place and your journey begins.

A Stroke of Meaningfulness

During a recent trip to Cape Town a friend paid me a wonderful compliment. He asked, 'Don't you ever stop engaging with people, telling them how happy you are to see them when you meet them, or asking them some sort of question?' Come to think of it, he might have been a bit irritated by this habit of mine, but it felt good to be able to make the connection and, in some way, establish a meaningful interaction.

HOW TO CREATE MEANING

'Once you know how, there are no more excuses.'

How to create meaning

It is an undisputed fact that meaning must be created. The blank canvas and multiple opportunities remain latent until the Meaning Maker engages with them. Through the individual's engagement and activation meaning is created.

In this, the most practical part of the book, the two separate but integral aspects – the internal condition and the external process – fuse to manifest meaningful and significant

experiences.

As they say, nothing happens until something moves. This is also true of the process of meaning creation. The tiniest shift of thought, intention, words or actions can bring about a chain reaction leading to the manifestation of a meaningful event. As the Meaning Maker one should certainly be aware and seek opportunities to put the process in motion, not only for one's own benefit but for the benefit of all.

The two processes involved in creating meaning focus on the internal world and the external world.

The internal conditions

These conditions are not exclusively reserved for the creation of meaning. To the contrary, these elements are proven practices that prepare fertile ground for life itself. As we go through them you will feel the value inherent in them and how they can assist and facilitate personal growth.

Silence

The argument continues: Which is more important, the notes of the music or the silence between the notes? Perhaps we should declare a draw. Notes without silence result in one long noisy affair and silence without notes is not music.

In a modern urban world, where the number of sensory stimuli we are exposed to increases daily, silence is often a blissful relief. We hear, see, feel, taste and smell so much that the brain becomes overloaded. There are just too many stimuli to process in too short a time. Silence gives us time to digest information, balance the mind, bring peace to the soul and rejuvenate us.

The value of silence is emphasised, though not always observed, in all cultural, religious and spiritual practices. In a mad, rushed world it takes special dedication for individuals to devote time to spend in silence. In a life filled with significance, balance is important and making time for the self, and spending some of that time in silence, is essential.

Vision

'I have a dream ...' Thus begins the speech that shaped the resistance movement in the USA and cemented Martin Luther King (Jr) in the minds of many generations. The principle is simple: If you can see the future, it's almost certain that you can create it. When talking about vision, the crux is one's ability and willingness to take time to create the future before you get there.

It is just so much easier to create a meaningful life if you can visualise what this life should look like, what process would be involved in achieving it, what behaviours you would like to demonstrate and how you see your life playing out. The more detailed your vision the better, and the more feeling you can add to your vision the better the chances that you will not quit before you realise that vision.

A meaningful vision will create a meaningful future.

Reflection

Taking time to reflect is always a good idea as it gives you perspective on your life. It could form part of your silent time or you can dedicate some specific time to reflect.

To reflect means to look back at events and find some meaning in them. The key to successful reflection is not to go into selfpity mode or apportioning blame either to yourself or others.

Reflection should involve as much detachment as possible as you look back on what was, how it happened and the role you and others played in these events in order to give some perspective to your life from the vantage point of distance.

During this time of reflection it is very easy to fall into the trap of pity and blame. The objective is perspective and one gains perspective by being as objective as humanly possible while remaining as unattached as one's ego will allow one to be.

Remember, you are not looking for a solution or a way to fix something; you are merely reflecting upon what has happened.

A Stroke of Meaningfulness

Years ago a very good friend and I crossed swords about a few issues and he wrote me an email saying I had deceived him and added that, in his opinion, I think

I am the god of Parkhurst (the suburb we live in). This perturbed me and for many months during which I reflected on what I had done wrong and how I could rectify the situation. Through reflection time I was able to find a way to make amends and rekindle the friendship.

Mindfulness

This may well be the single most important factor in the whole book – perhaps because without mindfulness all will be forgotten. This book eventually will end up on the bookshelf in the same way that an exercise bike ends up in the spare room or the garage. The intention will remain merely an intention and the action required to create significance will never be more than just thoughts or words. Mindfulness forces us to consciously strive towards a particular way of living with some broad concepts top of mind in order for it not to end up as the item on the to-do list without a tick.

For a whole year one of the companies I worked with made an in-house personal assistant available to me who was in charge of scheduling my appointments. For the whole year,

whenever I spoke to groups, I emphasised how important it is to show appreciation to the people who support you – to keep them in mind when you take staff out to lunch, to express your gratitude towards what they do and how they do it. Yet not once did I practise what I preached! For some insane reason

I was not mindful that this lady, paid by the customer but dedicated to my needs, could do with some appreciation – shocking! I just wasn't mindful at all.

Mindfulness will help you say 'thank you' to the security guard at the gate, it will help you remember to take flowers home, to not lose your temper with the shop assistant who is trying to help you, to call your parents or family to say 'I love you', to say sorry when you have made a mistake, to lend a hand when it is needed ...

Meaningfulness relies on mindfulness for its existence.

Without mindfulness nothing we learn will be put into practice – the good manners, the skills, the knowledge and the ability to act in a meaningful way will all fall by the wayside.

There are not enough words to describe the value of having a mindset that says, 'I want a meaningful life' and being mindful in creating it moment by moment.

The external process

When you go grocery shopping, you will often find that household cleaning items occupy the most space in your trolley, followed by raw foods that one must cook to create meals while the smallest part of you purchase consists of snack foods that you can eat right away such as bread, cheese, a packet of biscuits or perhaps some fruit. Well, the external process can be compared to that portion of your grocery shopping that you can consume immediately. Similarly, you can try every element in this section of the book right away.

The most wonderful thing is that each element will give you immediate meaningful results. The gratification these elements provide is thus instantaneous.

Many of my training sessions and seminars are only about these elements purely because they make an immediate difference to the quality and significance of one's life.

A while ago, just before a seminar, a media person who was present had voiced the opinion that all the aspects covered by speakers and trainers in the field of human potential are theoretical, non-practical and, to use his words, 'a bit fluffy'.

He had gone further and had challenged my claim that if you use these elements, your life will already have become more significant even before you pass through the security gate when you leave your home. I assured him that it was not an empty claim and that he was welcome to sit in and test the claim for himself. A few hours later, this initially sceptical man called to say that the claim was indeed true. You can expect the same result.

Here is how we create a meaningful life from an external point of view.

Self-expression

The reason we love art, music, the movies, talk shows, and so on is because we can identify with the expression these provide.

Everyone will agree that a picture is worth a thousand words because when looking at a picture, a painting or a sculpture we can project our own thoughts and emotions onto it. It is the same with music. For example, we love songs about love as they often express exactly how we feel and what the artist creates through notes or words often captures what we want to say.

Have you ever been involved in an argument or confrontation where the other person fails to listen to what you're saying and keeps interrupting you and shutting you up? In that situation, your initial feelings of frustration often translate into anger. If you are repeatedly not given the opportunity

to air your opinion, especially when it comes to intimate or long-term relationships, the anger can eventually lead to at best despondency and at worst depression. It is therefore of vital importance that we find ways and means to express ourselves. This expression can come in a variety of forms, for example, in verbal and non-verbal communication, working in the garden, painting, singing, playing with your children, watching sport with a friend and many more.

Following are a few basic pointers in self-expression to take note of. These will enhance the expression and make the experience of significance more real.

*** Self-confidence**
During my school days the one thing I lacked was the confidence to express myself. I grew up as an only child and although I had the ability to express myself, I did not have the confidence. The lack of confidence has a ripple effect.

You may have a point of view, the answers to questions, the solution to a problem, the talent or skills to make a difference, but without the confidence to express these you will become frustrated, inhibited and angry. This, in turn, will affect your levels of self-worth and self-esteem resulting in a negative downward spiral that will hold you back even more. Unless you can develop enough self-confidence to express yourself, the ripple effect of this vicious circle will continue.

In many cultures, including my own, women have, in the past, been discouraged from expressing themselves freely. Standing on stage, addressing the masses, speaking at weddings – all of these were once the exclusive preserve of men. Hence the level of self-confidence of many women did not develop as rapidly as that of their male counterparts. This is significant because the one sure way to build self-confidence is to continuously expose yourself to situations that demand self-expression and in this way to slowly nurture the development of this ability.

For any person to make a difference, to bring about change, to create meaning, expression is an integral part of the process. It is for this reason that we need to gradually work on our levels of self-confidence.

*** Verbal and non-verbal communication**
It is not what you say, but how you say it! We can say the same thing in a different tone of voice and elicit a completely different reaction. The reason your mother told you to count to ten before you speak is simple; she wanted you to think about how you were going to say what you wanted to say.

The words 'I love you' or 'I am sorry' are important, but not nearly as important as to how you say them. In fact, said in the wrong tone of voice, they could have exactly the opposite effect of what they are intended to convey.

The non-verbal area of communication is just as important.

Here again, a number of factors come into play, such as culture, customs, previous conditioning and general mindset. While lecturing years ago, I thought it well to tell my students that it was very bad manners to enter my office and then take a seat before I had invited them to do so. A black student shyly put up his hand and explained to me that, in his culture, it is a sign of respect to assume a subordinate position by not appearing taller than the older or more respected person in the room, and this was the reason for some students taking a seat in my office without first asking for permission to do so. This action would have continued to offend me if I hadn't been told about this custom inherent in his culture.

In certain cultures, making (and maintaining) eye contact and showing 'presence' during a conversation are considered good manners. In other cultures this is considered arrogant and disrespectful. It is of vital importance to familiarise yourself with these various non-verbal cues in order to facilitate meaningful interaction.

When walking into a convenience store it is not difficult to tell the difference between a sales assistant who is not in the mood to serve you and one who is. All you have to do is read their body language. Without one word being spoken, one can pick up a mood. In similar fashion, my mother could gauge my dad's mood when he entered our home after work.

The science of body language and non-verbal expression is astonishingly interesting. When we learn how to use it to our advantage and how to read it in other people, we grow in our ability to have meaningful communication.

*** Know your audience**
Whenever my father phones me and I am busy, I can say, 'Dad I can't speak right now', put the phone down and know that he won't take offence because he'll be pleased by the fact his son is busily engaged in doing business. When my mother calls, however, it is a totally different story. My mother is sensitive and emotional; I would never be short with her. I know this and for me to have a meaningful relationship with both of them I know how to treat them as individuals.

If you want a meaningful conversation you have to evaluate the person you are speaking to, adapt your style of communication and make sure that you make the connection.

Think about the person you are expressing yourself to and consider aspects such as:

- What kind of connections you have had with this person in the past
- The culture and background of the person
- The emotional state of the person
- The person's levels of exposure to and familiarity with what you are going to talk about
- The overall mental state of the person who may, for example, be nervous, in a hurry or otherwise occupied at that moment

This will help you to have the most meaningful conversation with him or her.

*** Analytical conversations**
Small talk is nice and we all love to engage in a bit of chitchat now and them. There is absolutely nothing wrong with that. Yet to develop meaningful self-expression one must have a circle of friends or acquaintances where there is also debate on significant topics from time to time. The more opportunities you have to state your point of view, take cognisance of someone else's and fence with words, the more you hone your communication skills.

Within this 'circle' of friends you start to grow as a thinker and your self-confidence grows because you are in a 'safe' group. Analytical conversation is vital to growth; it gives other people the opportunity to challenge your thinking as you challenge theirs. Through analytical conversation we begin to find meaningful solutions for some of the BIG issues of our time and thus become Meaning Makers.

Herewith you have the first element with which to create meaning. You can put this book down and choose to express yourself differently. The moment you do that, you can expect a different and more meaningful result.

A Stroke of Meaningfulness

A client told me about the most wonderful lesson he had learned from his son. When this boy, their first child, was born, he was diagnosed as mentally disabled.

My client – who admitted that he had never been comfortable with hugging and showing affection – described how he had struggled to relate to the boy.

He expressed his frustration in not being able to communicate with him and the boy's inability to express his needs. Yet he soon realised that his son was able to express his emotional needs

through physical touch and needed to be physically close to his father in order for them to communicate. Now, when he gets home from work, this father lies on the floor with his son and they hug and play until a quiet level of understanding and contentment sets in.

The magic – and it really is magic – is that we all have a need to find some means of expression for our abilities, talents, thoughts, and emotions. When we acquire the confidence, the skills and the ability to connect, we truly experience ourselves as being much more significant than we did previously. We feel that we are in conversation with our world and this conversation contributes greatly to our self-awareness and our sense of self-worth.

Involvement

There was a time in South Africa when all young men had to serve two years of compulsory military training. The only choice was to undergo this training either before or after completing one's tertiary education. The penalty for failing to do so was a three-year jail sentence.

Having completed my studies, I therefore duly reported for my two years of military training. Needless to say, both I and my fellow conscripts would much rather have entered the labour market and become economically active at that stage.

My mindset was negative and my attitude was just to get my military training over and done with. I was assigned to Human Resources reporting to a wonderful colonel. After many long conversations, I realised a profound practical truth: to have a meaningful experience and for the sake of your own sanity and state of mind you need to get involved. The more involved you are, the greater the chances that you will have a good time and, in some miraculous way, the more involved you are, the more quickly the time goes by. I changed my mindset, got involved in my work and gave of my best. My dreaded military training turned out instead to be a great

learning experience with a lot of meaningful encounters that facilitated a good deal of personal growth.

Have you ever noticed how slowly time passes when you are not involved in your work? You look at your watch and it is 12:00 pm. When you look again, after what feels like two hours later, it is only 2:15 pm. Time stands still when you are not involved. Everyone I know would rather have a busy day than wait impatiently for the time to pass.

Involvement is literally the activation of meaning. The moment you choose to get up, step up and get involved, benefits come your way. It's all good and well to plan and fantasise about what you are going to do, but the value definitely lies in the doing. The opposite of involvement is isolation and, as you can imagine, if you isolate yourself you significantly reduce your chances of creating meaning. You cannot practise self-expression and you cannot add value in isolation.

Non-involvement also gives rise to the possibility of seeking diversion through non-mindful activities which can result in frustration, negativity and heartache. It is fairly easy to become drawn into negative involvement which drains your energy rather than boosting it. How often do we look forward to a dinner party or a get-together only to find our friends and associates whining about the weather, the economy, the cost of living, the potholes in our roads and so on? By the time we leave, we are exhausted by all the negativity. The secret is to choose what you get involved in and to put your energy in the most positive places.

You may also often find that, although you are not necessarily involved in negative stuff, you are also not involved in projects and social interaction that add value. The solution to this is volunteering. The word 'volunteering' is unfortunately often negatively associated with something that nobody really wants to do, but somebody has to do it. Change your perception about volunteering!

Volunteering can change your life. If you are self-aware you will know what it is that gives pleasure and adds meaning to your life. The next step is to actively seek projects where you can offer your skills and abilities for the benefit of others.

The rewards are massive. These projects can be found at your workplace, within your community, your family, local government structures – literally anywhere that you feel that what you have to offer is needed. This could also well be a project you have personally initiated and, by getting other like-minded people involved, you offer them the benefit of creating meaning in their lives.

Finally, the truth is that isolation will not bring you meaning.

The only way you can manifest meaning in your life is to become positively involved. The world needs you, not to do nothing, but to get involved in something significant. This something will reveal itself to you when you take the time to be silent. Once you know what it is that you want to get involved in, you are ready to discover the meaningful role you can play and the positive contribution you can make. At the end of your life, you will then not look back with regret at the things you haven't done, but with pride at the things you have done and you will be content.

Contribution

I have a sign on my wall that reads: 'Commit Random Acts of Kindness'. I have engraved in my consciousness a desperate need to make a difference in life, and the one thing I know for sure is that if you commit acts of kindness and if you actively strive to make a difference to the lives of others, you will forever have a life filled with meaning.

In our quest to be more productive, achieve higher efficiencies and build a sustainable economy, our success or otherwise

A Stroke of Meaningfulness

At OR Tambo Airport I recently met a young student who was on his way to Cape Town to go back to school. His mother, who lives in Limpopo – approximately a four-hour drive from Johannesburg – had booked his flight online. The airline insisted that the credit-card holder be present in order to validate the ticket before he could board the flight. With his mother in Limpopo, that was not going to happen. He either had to take a taxi back to Limpopo or book and pay for another flight which was also impossible. I asked him who he was waiting for and he told me that his mother had told him to just stand there and wait because an angel would be coming to help him. After I successfully interceded with the airport's management on his behalf, he came to me and asked, 'Are you an angel, sir?' I smiled and said, 'We all are!'

is evaluated in terms of certain key performance indicators, productivity targets and many other standards. The higher one's need to add value and to make a difference, the better one's chances of meeting all of these standards that are put in place to evaluate output.

There is an argument that postulates that if you follow your bliss, find your purpose and are passionate about your work, you will make a difference, be content in your field of endeavour and reach your targets. The challenge comes about when you are in a job towards which you have no strong feelings and therefore little drive to succeed. How then do you remain motivated, reach targets and make a difference?

The answer is that you can do what you love or you can love what you do. It is very possible to focus on the effect you can have on the business and really get to love what you do.

The more you focus on the value you add, the difference you can make, the efficiencies you can introduce in the way you carry out your tasks, the more you will love what you do and the easier it will become to maintain your motivation and productivity. Nor need you have any fear of not measuring up to the performance indicators that have been set because you will be fully engaged in your work. Contribution also has to do with giving. This refers not only to the giving of money and what money can buy. More often it refers to giving of love, respect, support, kindness, understanding, a shoulder to cry on and an ear to listen.

It has been proven over and over that the greatest reward does not go to the receiver, but to the giver. There is immediate gratification in contribution. The second we open our hearts to give, we are at that very moment experiencing ourselves as useful and meaningful.

At the age of eighty-five, when my dad visits my home, he walks around the house, commenting on the state of the garden, the rising damp on the walls and anything else he can find wrong.

Years ago I interpreted this as criticism and it used to anger me, but I now know that, in his old age, he is merely looking for a way to still be of some use, to be able to add value and make a difference.

We do not come to earth to partake only in the four 'f's' – fight, flight, feed and fornication – despite the fact that nowadays many works of fiction, movies, documentaries, radio and television broadcasts tend to place a great deal of emphasis on these basic instincts. Although the four f's are an inextricable part of the human condition, our consciousness has evolved beyond them towards the higher purpose of making a difference. We think more, feel more

A Stroke of Meaningfulness

Perhaps the givers of love, kindness, respect, money and all the things the world needs, know best when they say that giving is a sure way of knowing that you are meaningful. What you give to one of us, you give to all of us – definitely something to consider if we want to succeed in changing our world.

deeply, experience more broadly. We are more aware of the importance of our soul's journey than purely our physical survival and the propagation of the species. It is for these reasons that we should live less selfish lives and make the greatest possible difference while we walk this earth. Herein lies the key to experiencing ourselves as more significant.

Non-judgement

Since we live on a planet where time and space are of the essence, it is impossible not to judge. For everything there is an equal opposite. The one cannot exist without the other – each shade of dark has its equivalent opposite shade of light, all distances have equal opposites and so do degrees of good and evil, old and young, sweet and sour, etc.

The mind finds its holding position by judging anything and everything against its equal opposite. For example, you are a male only in relation to the opposite gender which is female or vice versa; you can only consider yourself to be strong compared with what you evaluate to be weak. This is not only true for the extremes of white and black, but also for all the shades of grey in between – hence our judgemental mind.

While we are here on earth we have unique opportunities to experience the separateness in all variations and to realise that in separation there is only one solution and that is to bring the two halves together in an attempt to lessen our perception of separateness and enhance our understanding of the whole and oneness. The more we move away from the separateness (judgement) towards the oneness (non judgement) the more evolved and conscious we become.

Our ability to judge is necessary for our survival and we do no harm by being able to tell when it is day and when

it is night. Unfortunately, this is not where our tendency to judge stops. Rather, we take this ability to distinguish and apply it in other areas of our lives – sometimes with very negative consequences. For example, we develop different behaviours towards those we judge as being the opposite of ourselves resulting in an emphasis on our differences as human beings rather than on our similarities. We begin to act out this negative behaviour towards those things, ways and people who do not look and behave as we do. Sooner or later we find more people like us who support our judgemental attitudes and beliefs. We then form cohesive groups and begin to create the group belief that those who do not fit the profile 'our people' must be one of 'them' and 'they' must be eliminated and marginalised as they pose a threat to our thinking and behaviour. Racial, social, religious and gender discrimination are only a few of the negative consequences arising from this erroneous belief. Surely you can by now see where this is going.

Through our thinking and behaviour we begin to be fearful of anything and everything that might intrude on or challenge our customs and way of life. We soon begin to perceive this as a threat to our collective identity and respond by marginalising those who are different from us in an attempt to preserve our ways and to continue to enjoy the benefits of these.

The logical correlatives of this fear manifest as greed. We are prepared to rape the earth in order to acquire enough oil to sustain our industrialised way of life; we think nothing of feeding harmful substances to animals in order to increase meat production; we deplete our natural vegetation in a misguided effort to extract maximum value from it over and above our need for food; we invade and occupy land because we are afraid if we don't, someone else will, and then we will suffer. We will even go so far as killing one another to maintain this notion that our way is the 'right' and only way.

Our fear drives us to obtain more, to own more, to extract more, without regard for those without the means to do the same. This is based on Darwin's notion of 'the survival of the fittest' taken to an extreme and unsustainable degree.

We misinterpret the ancient spiritual writings, build churches, temples, mosques, synagogues and preach the virtues of our beliefs as often as people are willing to listen in an attempt to convince the masses that 'our' way is the right way.

The worst consequence of this is the possibility that we will condition generation after generation to keep this 'value system' intact and thereby fill them with the fear that if they don't, they will suffer. We have bought into the illusion of separateness and we are more filled with fear than with love.

The fact remains, however, that for us to be meaningful and significant, we need love and not fear.

You may well ask how we can escape millennia of separateness and fear and move towards oneness and love. The answer lies in our essence which is love. The world will be a better place when you and I can look at one another knowing we are different and use that differentness as a tool to learn from, become a better and wiser person in the process, and thank the other for providing an example of that equal opposite

from whom we can learn so much.

This may be the biggest challenge in the process of meaning making – to operate from a position of non-judgement and love. If we can do this, if we can promote and foster oneness amongst each other, we will truly become Meaning Makers and the reward will be love.

I know that the solution seems to be too simple and too onedimensional for such a complex problem, but it is not. We are the ones who have complicated the problem so that we can perpetuate the fear and create the illusion that it is too difficult for one of us to even attempt to solve. Yet the solution is simple: Live from a place of love and the rest will follow.

Curiosity

A friend of mine's father, Mr Venter, is a man with whom I have a lot of contact because I am so intrigued by his way of thinking and doing. At age eighty-one he still plays golf, reads up on sport and has a professional golf coach. Both his sons live abroad and he wanted to be able to communicate with them efficiently online so, at the age of about sixty-something he enrolled to do a diploma in Information Technology and would make the hour's drive from Scottborough on the South Coast to Durban to attend classes. He is very proud of his

insatiable curiosity about life.

Those serious about experiencing a significant life are also most definitely curious about life and how to maximise their

A Stroke of Meaningfulness

experience of it. As stated previously, we have all wondered about the meaning of life, what happens when we die, how we can make the best of our lives, how to grow old graciously, whether there is a God and whether he/she loves us, and any more questions. All these questions arise from curiosity.

Without it we would not have become more conscious, we would not have discovered the existence of continents other than our own and medical research, leading to significant breakthroughs in curing life-threatening ailments, would not have happened. Curiosity is essential to any kind of future.

Imagine if we all became curious enough about the big questions to begin to make a collective effort to explore

the answers. Some of these include who we are, how we are similar to and different from each other, how to work together to create a better life, how to end poverty, how to create wealth for all countries, how to avoid destroying the planet and how to sustain longevity on earth.

If all of this doesn't make you curious, use your quiet time and connectiveness to other people to spark your curiosity because, when your curiosity has taken off, your life begins to be purposeful and significant.

A few basic pointers in becoming more curious:

- Seek to find your essence.
- Ask questions beginning with 'who', 'why' and 'where'.
- Engage all sorts of people, especially if they are different from you.
- Don't accept the status quo.
- Know that all progress – especially yours – depends on curiosity.

In the midst of the information age, the satisfaction of curiosity has been enabled by the proverbial click of a button. You don't even have to leave your house or office to begin finding out more about your world and how to live in it. After you've done that, become curious about how your involvement could have an impact on this world.

Appreciation

If there is one thing that increases the value of the human experience, it must be appreciation. We all love to feel

appreciated as this serves as confirmation that we have made a difference and are living meaningful lives. No matter who you are or what you do, we all enjoy the feeling of being

appreciated.

I recently walked into a convenience store and, while paying for my purchases, watched the lady who was busy packaging them. She carefully packed the items into the plastic bags, making sure the heavy products were at the bottom. I complimented her by saying that I was glad she was the one doing the packing rather than me as I would have packed the milk on top of the bread and by the time I reached home

I would have had squashed bread. She laughed and said that one learns with time how to pack correctly. I thanked her again and left the store with my bags.

A Stroke of Meaningfulness

I once heard the story about a father who forbade his son from reading the books in the family's home library. He told his son that they were too difficult and he would in any case not understand what they were about. By age sixteen the boy admitted to his father that his curiosity had gotten the better of him, that he had secretly read all the books in the house and that they were not that difficult. The father admitted that his devious plan had worked!

A few days later, I returned to the same store and the same woman came to greet me. She said that she wanted to thank me for showing my appreciation the last time I was at the store. She told me that when she got home from work that day, she had told her two girls about the incident and they had both been so proud of her. She said that I had added such a lot of value to her life. I asked myself: Is that all it takes to make a difference in someone's life? And if it is, I really must be more mindful to look for every opportunity to express my appreciation of those around me.

In the book *The One Minute Manager*, Ken Blanchard says it is important to catch people doing something right. We are too often on the lookout for mistakes and react quickly when we catch someone doing something wrong in order to point out their mistake or to give advice. When we catch someone doing something right and show our appreciation, we are reinforcing positive behaviour which creates a feeling of significance and pride within the individual. In this way we encourage positive behaviour.

It is equally important to appreciate the role you play in your work and personal life.

When you reflect upon your week, month or year, give yourself credit and be proud of the difference and the contribution you have made. This internal appreciation serves as a great self-motivation tool and increases one's feelings of self-worth.

Take the time to appreciate the contribution others have made to your life and find ways to show them how much you appreciate their involvement in your life. This will encourage them to continuously make positive contributions to the lives of the people they come into contact with.

Following are a few basic ways to show appreciation.

- Put a smile on your face and use positive non-verbal gestures to express your appreciation.
- Use verbal expressions such as 'thank you', 'I appreciate', 'well done', 'it means a lot to me', etc.
- Close the loop – when in a conversation make sure you close the loop and acknowledge the other party's involvement in the conversation.
- Allow people to shine. Be mindful to allow other people to take the limelight, to shine and to feel valued.
- Make that call. In other words, take the time to take action. Give your family members a call, tell your friends what they mean to you, acknowledge the security guard – through these gestures you show that you live a connected life within which everyone matters and is appreciated.
- Connect – show people that you are for real and that they matter to you. When you interact, make the connection.

This connection shows others that you respect and appreciate them.

Appreciation is a wonderful tool to increase your own selfworth and that of others as it confirms that we are Meaning Makers and that we all, in our own way, make a difference in life.

This then takes care of the external process. These elements you can put into practice right away and there will be an immediate proportional increase in your experience of meaningfulness and significance. The best part is that when you begin to do these simple things – which, after all, cost nothing and constitute no more than an acknowledgement of our common humanity – you will become progressively more conscious of areas where you can improve. You will also soon derive a great deal of pleasure and meaning from these habits and your behaviour will bear testimony to an individual who is mindful of living a meaningful life.

A Stroke of Meaningfulness

At a conference where I had been invited to speak, the exiting managing director of PEP Stores, George Steyn

mentioned in his farewell speech that he had received a note from a staff member that had said: 'You will forever be my favourite person because, when I sat next to you last year, you took the time to find out what is important to me and you even remembered my name.'

THE INFLUENCES THAT IMPACT MEANING

'Nothing exists in isolation. Everything is a function of everything else.'

The understanding and the conceptualisation of meaningfulness and significance are impacted by four major influences. At no point can meaning stand homogeneously alone. It is always modified by a number of influences. The following four influences contribute to the subjective experience of meaning. What each individual understands, and how this understanding fits into the selfgoverning system of the individual, depends largely on these influences.

Separately and collectively, these influences shape our experience of meaningfulness.

They are:

Values and beliefs

We cannot separate our behaviour from our values. The way we do things depends on our values. Our values are concepts and ideas which are the consequences of our beliefs. Our beliefs are always imparted to us from an external source such as upbringing, conditioning, experience, etc. They become part of our DNA and literally run our operating system. For instance, if you have the value of honesty you will have a deeper belief that cheating is wrong, that to always speak the truth is best, that it is wrong to mislead people and so forth. Thus the belief gives birth to the value.

If we accept that it is true that our behaviour is directed by our values, we must then also accept that how we will create meaning will also be affected by our values. Consider, for a moment, that how you express yourself, and how you exercise your judgement or non-judgement, are determined by your values. You can now see that all the internal and external ways of creating meaning are dependent on your personal

values and beliefs.

For a very long time I held the belief that one-to-one contact was superior to group contact. This gave rise to a value of personal connection. Yet this value held me back from appearing publicly and addressing large groups. Years later I had to re-examine my belief and my value in order to express myself to groups and thereby create meaning in my own life and the lives of others. By now you can feel both the positive and the negative power of beliefs and values in the process of creating meaning.

There are many disempowering beliefs that can constrain your ability to express yourself, get involved and create significance in your life. It is therefore important to constantly re-evaluate your beliefs and values in order to determine whether they empower or disempower you. If the latter, then challenge your beliefs and their origin and make

sure your meaningfulness is not limited by a disempowering belief system.

Religion

Religion or dogma is a combination of belief (theism) and knowledge (gnostic) and has a profound impact on how we experience ourselves as meaningful. Because of the divinity involved in religion our beliefs and values as dictated by religion come from a higher source, compelling us to adhere to them more stringently. This, of course, affects our behaviour and our experience of meaning. Even when it comes to logic and humanism, religious beliefs often override all the other beliefs and values. For example, one could argue that to kill someone is logically and morally unacceptable, thus upholding the value of life unless otherwise prescribed by religious writings or religious leaders.

The aspect of divinity and the rules set out by a higher force direct the behaviour of those who subscribe to a particular religion. For many believers, those religious guidelines spell out how to conduct oneself and how to live, who to side

with and who not to. These guidelines are specific in terms of how to live and what meaning and significance are all about.

Most important to know is that religious beliefs do influence and guide the behaviour of those who subscribe to them.

Therefore the meaningfulness and significance will be guided by the specifics of the religion.

If you are religious and of a specific faith, then try to find a way within the guidelines of your faith to create meaning, to judge as little as possible and to make a difference in the world you live in.

Consumption

The saying goes, 'As we think, so shall we be'. This is very true.

The deeper question is: What influences our thinking? If we can control the influences on our thinking we can guide our behaviour and – with reference to the saying quoted above – we can guide our 'being'. Isn't that exactly what creating meaning is all about? We want to 'BE' more meaningful.

To refer back to the first section of this book where we looked at the 'blank canvas', we agreed that the markings on the canvas create the picture. To use another metaphor, think of what happens when we consume positivity or significance.

The more positivity we consume the better the chances that we will transmit or produce more positivity.

Now you know where consumption as a factor that influences meaning is heading. The quality of the meaning we will be able to create will be directly proportional to the quality of that which we consume. Our responsibility then lies in checking and double checking the quality of what we allow the external world to feed us.

In the area of physical health it is said that 'you are what you eat and drink'. It works exactly the same way in the area of mental health. We consume mostly through our senses.

Hearing, vision, taste, feel, smell – all of these modalities have an impact on both our physical and mental health. If you take drugs, your ability to think clearly will be impaired and if you spend days on end with negative people or find yourself in a negative work or home environment, your attitudes, values and general sense of wellbeing will be at risk of being undermined.

We will have to become snobs when it comes to what we are

willing to consume on a physical and mental level. Reading the newspaper and watching the news help us to stay informed, but what are you doing to counteract the negativity you consume through the media? Are you keeping the bad news in perspective by also reading some positive material?

Do you hang out with people who are solution- rather than problem-orientated?

Our 'being' depends on consumption and we have free will to choose what we are going

to consume every moment of every day. If you, at some point, are at the mercy of a colleague, family member or friend who transmits negativity, take steps to actively neutralise the negativity

by consuming some positivity.

Your significance as a human (being) depends on it.

Adversity

'You don't know how strong you are until strong is the only option you have left.' This statement has always fascinated me, perhaps because one cannot imagine how one would get through a period of adversity until one is in it. Only then do you find the power to conquer.

There is a big reward for being strong, for holding on and getting through the tough times we are all faced with at certain points in our lives. The reward is personal growth. Yet this growth takes place at a different rate and in a different way during tough times compared with good times. Yes, one grows during the good times as well, but coping with those more difficult times in our lives is what builds strength of character.

We didn't come to earth, this planet of duality, to remain unaffected by what happens to us. We come here to learn and to grow. As someone once said to me, the worst thing that can happen to you is nothing. When something happens to us we grow and we love to grow. Most amazing is the fact that we are built for tough times. We are resilient. We don't perish easily and our spirits are stronger than we can ever imagine. Even our seemingly fragile bodies can take more that we give them credit for.

So it is a given that each one of us and those around us, whom we love and care for, will fall ill, will experience suffering and we will all die. Linked to this suffering will be some form of mental and emotional trauma which some will experience more acutely than others as we all experience and respond to trauma in a different way. There are three topics to consider.

Acceptance

The Buddha said that once you accept that life is suffering there will be no more suffering. In other words, once one accepts the situation, the process of moving through it becomes accelerated. It is when one remains in denial that the after effects become prolonged and extended. Acceptance lies in the acknowledgement of the truth and facing the reality of the situation. Acceptance is a very powerful and silent state within us. From here we can enter into a meaningful period of growth.

Faith

There are many definitions of faith that fit the context in which the world is one. The one part that stands out is that faith is a strong, unshakeable belief in something of which there is no proof or empirical evidence of its existence.

From a psychological point of view, faith focuses the mind on positivity and for this we do not need evidence or proof.

The value of faith in times of adversity is that although we cannot, with the logical mind, perceive goodness resulting from adversity, or learn the lesson that lies latent within it, or even the potential for growth that it offers, we do believe

(have faith) that all these things are there and that everything will work out for the best, whatever that may be.

Surrender

To surrender is not to give up; not at all. It is to go with acceptance and faith to an internal place of peace where

the ego and the personal will take a back seat to a greater picture and a greater power where things happen exactly the way they should and whichever way they turn out will be just

perfect.

Yes, adversity does contribute to creating a meaningful life and, as we know, with all the pleasant and not-so-pleasant things that will come to pass, helps us to become more conscious and more significant.

Values, religion, consumption and adversity are the four factors that have the most profound impact on meaning. Each plays a role in terms of which we as individuals think about and experience meaningfulness.

The key is to take cognisance of these four factors in one's own life and become mindful of how they impact human experience.

POSITIVE ENHANCERS OF MEANING

'The probability and possibility of meaning is always enhanced by positivity.'

Positive enhancers of meaning

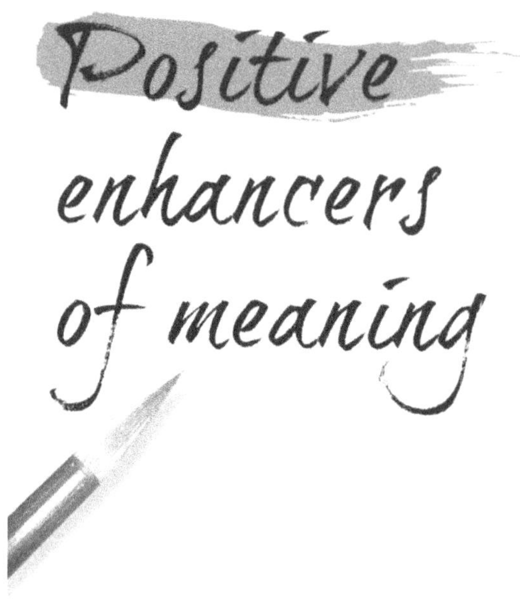

The taste of food fascinates me. I am never sure whether we really have consensus on taste. What is sweet for

me might be less sweet for you. Some people consider certain foods as delicacies while others pull their noses up at them. So it is hard to say what tastes grand and what doesn't.

At a dinner party I heard that pepper enhances the taste of some blends of tea, balsamic vinegar enhances the taste of strawberries and sugar makes tomatoes taste great. After trying these various taste combinations for myself, I must agree that they work well together.

In all facets of life there is something that increases the essence of the object or the activity. Candles contribute to a romantic atmosphere, exercise increases the feeling of wellbeing and so forth. It is not different when it comes to meaning. The following aspects increase or enhance the understanding and the experience of meaningfulness.

Patience

We all know the saying: 'If something is worthwhile it is worthwhile waiting for.' Life unfolds in its own time and

according to its own rhythm. In the same way that spring follows winter and dessert follows a main meal, meaning and patience are siblings where meaning follows patience.

Too often we push too hard because we have a timeframe within which to achieve certain goals and, no matter what the timeframe of the universe is, we want what we want when we want it while the universe insists that we will only get what we want when the time is right. By being impatient we can literally miss out on a meaningful experience or a life-changing experience. The best way to use patience to enhance meaningfulness is to become sensitive to the rhythm of all things around you and to be able to adjust your own rhythm to the greater rhythm of the things and events you are part of. This will heighten your experience of oneness and patience will become part of who you are.

Knowledge + experience = wisdom

These three elements should really be treated as three separate topics that enhance the experience of meaning

because it is a proven fact that wisdom comes about when you have acquired knowledge and experience. I have decided to combine them into a formula. This does not mean that the one is more or less important than the other. Towards the end of this section it will become clear to you how knowledge, experience and wisdom tangle and untangle both as single concepts and as a collective. Knowledge is something we can and do all acquire. This could come through lectures, reading, listening, watching, etc. The fact is that knowledge is specific information about a specific topic. In the information age in which we now find ourselves, the acquiring of knowledge has become so much easier.

According to its dictionary definition knowledge is information acquired through experience or education and includes both the theoretical and practical understanding of

A Stroke of Meaningfulness

I once had someone ask me whether I had a book or a program that might teach him patience. Instead I advised him to do the following simple exercise: One, you ask the universe to teach you patience; and two you ask your family to do the same. You will soon find that either the universe or a family member will, for example, have hidden your car keys when you are late for work and there you have a great opportunity to practise patience – you will either get it, or then again, you might not.

the subject. Not being a linguist at all, my opinion may not count for much. Having said that, allow me to disagree with the definition. Knowledge in a more metaphysical context is information acquired through an educational process and doesn't include a practical or a high skills component. This does not mean for a second that knowledge is less important than experience or wisdom. Knowledge is essential to the enhancement of one's understanding of meaning. The more educated you become on a particular topic by reading books like this one and interacting with people who have knowledge, experience and wisdom, the deeper your level of knowledge will become.

It is an absolute fact that the more knowledge and understanding you have on any topic, the more potential power you have to master it. I would therefore encourage you to develop an unquenchable thirst for knowledge; it will serve you all your life and not only enrich your own life, but also those of the people who deal with you.

Experience, as you know, cannot be bought. It cannot be faked and it is a priceless commodity in the world of meaning.

As a young consultant I couldn't wait to lose some hair, get a few grey ones or even a few wrinkles to show some outward signs that I'd been around the block a time or two and gained some experience because experience gives one just that little bit more respect. Yes, the paper trail of certificates you earn though education are there for all to see, but to be able to back that up with experience is what you really want.

It would be fair to say that experience equals time and that is something you cannot fast-track. If one thinks back to involvement, the key might just be in the fact that the more involved you become in meaningful pursuits, the more experience you will gain. One's willingness to acquire experience is really so important. It is this mindset that might, for example, motivate you to volunteer and give of your time to a particular cause because you know that somewhere down the line it will pay off.

During the 11th century AD the alchemist became known as a special and talented person who could change base metals into gold. Later on this term was adopted to refer to businessmen and others who could fuse disparate elements in such a way as to bring about a very positive result. Using the same model, if we fuse knowledge and experience, we end up with wisdom. Yes, a very special attribute usually

associated with a long-bearded individual with a walking stick and a quizzical expression on the face.

Wisdom does not belong exclusively to the old guard however. Yes, the time factor in gaining experience does suggest that age has something to do with acquiring it as explained in the previous paragraphs. Yet wisdom belongs to all those who are willing to integrate both knowledge and experience and are tenacious in their efforts to constantly grow as human beings.

Perhaps more than money, more than status and more than respect from others, the one thing that will serve us and the people we interact with is wisdom. There will come a time when your friends, colleagues, family members and children will turn to you for advice. The quality of this advice and the ability to make a meaningful contribution to their lives will depend on the level of wisdom you have attained. Whenever you learn and/or experience something new, remember that this will be added to the alchemist's melting pot to be used at a later stage in the form of wisdom.

Insight

When you have the opportunity to watch knowledge, experience and wisdom in action, you can almost feel the magnificent power of insight being demonstrated. As the word suggests, insight is the ability to see below the surface – to be able to factor a number of issues, facts, opinions or data into the equation and extrapolate from this some deeper meaning, some pattern that not everyone can see.

When Nelson Mandela was released from prison he analysed the situation in South Africa. He had the difficult task of striking a balance between the expectations of the oppressed and the fears of the oppressors. Because of the way he handled this situation, he will forever be seen as an icon of wisdom through his insight into the psyche of all the groups in the country. His insight spared us a bloody revolution, lack of confidence in our future in the international arena and a total collapse of the economy. There are many great examples of insight. This one happened under our noses and affected everyone who lives on the African continent.

If you analyse all the good-news stories, whether in book form, audio or on screen, you will almost always find that a positive turn of events has to do with insight. The truth is that insight is a bit like the naked truth that reveals itself the minute someone points it out, the minute someone assembles and analyses all the information to provide a deeper understanding of the situation. Ordinary people just cannot ignore it. It brings a whole new dimension to the problem or situation and, in some way, it provides not only a solution but also brings hope and some form of emotional victory.

The gardener, builder, plumber, doctor, housewife, teacher – everyone who has knowledge, experience and wisdom in their field – has the ability to show insight and the more they

A Stroke of Meaningfulness

When I was younger I harboured the innocent belief that everyone wants to do the right thing by their fellow man, and that no one will cheat you or do you harm, especially if you show them that you yourself are the real deal. I had to learn over time that there are ducks and eagles and that if it walks like a duck, quacks like a duck, it is a duck and not an eagle.

actually practise it, the better their chances of developing further and deeper insight. The same applies to life. Insight into life and life's challenges is not reserved for philosophers and professors but is available to everyone who can truly connect with what lies beneath the superficial appearance of a problem or situation and bring forth a unique perspective on it or way of meeting the challenge.

Insight has the magnificent attribute of enhancing one's experience of significance as it always carries within it the

potential for uniqueness.

Context

When my mother tells me that at birth I was the most beautiful infant in the hospital, this needs to be seen in context. My parents were married for thirteen years before I was born, the birth took place in a small town and in an even smaller hospital and, to top it all, she had a cesarean delivery. So, as you can see, to be able to make anything of her observation, one needs to give context to her remark.

Another example could be the statement that, from an economic point of view, life is tough at the moment, which is true and there is nothing wrong with such a statement. To give context to it one would also have to state that one third of the world's population is unemployed, in many countries people live on less than one US$ per day, some countries have been locked in war for a long time and there are many homeless and also very unhealthy people in the world. With this as background, the statement that life is tough becomes relative to the context of the hardships being experienced by citizens of other countries and casts a different light on what

'tough' really means.

The ability to give context to any situation depends largely on the ability to distance oneself from one's own situation in order to gain a clearer and more balanced perspective, and to be able to take into consideration a number of other factors that relate to one's specific situation which can add a deeper perspective.

Usually, the people who are good at bringing context to a situation or a challenge are those who can detach themselves from their emotional involvement, get some distance, apply insight and pull together a number of factors relevant to the situation.

If one really wants to be able to apply context in life, a wonderful contributing factor is to have had the opportunity to travel – the more widely the better. The more one is exposed to other ways of thinking, other cultures, other religions and ways of living, the easier it becomes to place one's own life within a wider context.

While it is true that knowledge aids one's understanding of context, it has been found that experience is a far more significant contributor to the area of contextualisation.

Often people state how hard they work and this is undoubtedly true until, for example, you spend eight hours two kilometres down a mine. When you surface you will have a completely different insight into what hard work means.

Another important contributing factor to the ability to conceptualise must be Einstein's theory of relativity.

Everything on the planet is relative – from suffering, hard work, being happy, to making a difference. Relativity gives us perspective and the ability to gently breathe out the stress and over-involvement in our own situation as we contextualise this within the bigger picture.

Questioning

Having grown up in a Calvinistic environment, in my case questioning was not high on the list of priorities when

a child or young person was taught how to relate to the external world. The virtues that were considered to be highly important were respect, acceptance, faith and a few more which, in themselves, are great virtues to have.

However, for many people brought up within an environment where questioning is actively discouraged in favour of blind faith, the issue becomes more complex. For these people, questioning becomes very uncomfortable for two reasons.

Firstly, to question is considered morally reprehensible in certain contexts and secondly, when they dare to do so, the answers they receive or the conclusions they may reach on their own may contradict what they have learned as children to accept as absolute truths. This sets up cognitive dissonance within the individual, which may be defined as an uncomfortable mental state resulting from conflicting perceptions, intuition, knowledge and reasoning.

Only much later in life did I begin to understand that the value of all virtues must be tested by one's own conviction. This process of testing can only take place through experience or learning the art of questioning. In other words, when you pay respect to a respectable person this behaviour is correct and the virtue is reinforced. On the other hand, when you pay respect to a non-respectable person you will have learned through experience that not all people are deserving of the same kind of respect.

For the Meaning Maker it is important to question the value of respect and to debate this with the self or others. Questioning does not indicate a lack of faith, respect or any other virtue; we question because of a deeper need

to understand and find context for a situation or type of behaviour.

The Buddha was adamant that one should not believe anything he or any other teacher has to offer until or unless

that teaching sits well with you and gives you inner peace – in other words until the teaching or virtue becomes truth in your life.

This is precisely the value of questioning. You need to assume a neutral mindset and ask critical questions about the subject until you gain enough relevant information for you to be comfortable with the subject so that you may internalise and then live it with conviction.

The most powerful way to approach the art of questioning is to say to yourself, 'I don't know anything about this' and then ask questions such as: 'What is this all about?' 'What does it mean and what is clouding my judgement?' 'How can I look at this differently?' By continuing this line of questioning and doing so with an open mind with the intention of really fostering a better understanding, you will find new dimensions within yourself, the subject and/or the behaviour you are questioning.

Fun, laughter and light-heartedness

The philosopher Lao Tzu, the author of *Tao Te Ching* who was born 604 BC said that it may not be such a great idea to ponder the meaning of life before age 50. He also said that even when you do ponder those more serious questions in life – such as the meaning of life and why things are the way they are – it is advisable to maintain a sense of spontaneity and light-heartedness. I think that what he really wanted to

say was: Have some fun.

I have had the pleasure and privilege of being in the presence of two of the world's most prominent spiritual teachers, namely the Dalai Lama and Bishop Desmond Tutu.

Apart from the obvious, which is that both these men have true substance and are dedicated to their calling in life, the one thing that stands out about both of them is their childlike happiness and playfulness. It is almost as if they have a built-in authentic and genuine smile that comes from their souls and manifests on their faces. When you are in their presence you cannot help experiencing their infectious joy and sharing in their free spirits. Perhaps these qualities are what we often fail to bring to our investigation of the 'serious' things in life.

At school my best friend was a guy by the name of Vivian.

Thinking back on our times together I remember two things – how we laughed and laughed about almost everything and the long hours he gladly put into helping me with maths. Vivian now lives in Portugal but we call each other a few times a year and guess what? At the end of every conversation I feel as if I have done a thousand sit-ups because my tummy muscles ache from all the laughter we share each time.

Scientists know for a fact that when you laugh your brain produces the happy hormones that help to cure illness and strengthen your immune system. It would thus be foolish not to include fun and laughter as an important element that enhances the experience of meaning and significance.

Perhaps we shouldn't take life or ourselves too seriously and perhaps we should approach the good and not-so-good times with a smile on our faces because we know for a fact that at times life will deal us an ace and at other times the Joker. The secret could therefore be to keep smiling because in the next round, everything might change.

In the area where we live there is a homeless lady who walks the streets of Rosebank and Parkhurst. She carries two large bags and is known as 'the bag lady'. She talks to herself continually and has an ever-so-slight smile on her face. I have often wondered whether perhaps she knows something that

we don't.

These positive enhancers of meaning are, in a way, the spices of life; on their own they are not nearly as powerful as when used in the context of the events and situations we face in life. Think about them in the same way as you think about any spice – the key is to find the right amount to use in the dish of life, not to overpower but rather to positively enhance. As with everything in life, the more often an enhancer of meaning is used, the higher the levels of familiarity with it and soon, like spice, it will fuse with the commonplace events of life and become an integral part of the 'dish'.

CONNECTIVE BEHAVIOUR

'Only through our connectedness to others can we really know the self and, as we enhance the self, the connectedness to others improves.'

Connective behaviour

In the final analysis, there is a generic answer to the question: 'What is the meaning of life?' The conclusion

will have to be that it is all about 'waking up', attaining a higher level of consciousness and developing, maintaining and observing connective behaviour in the world you live in.

Connective behaviour equals significance! Whether you are on your way to work, at work, spending time alone, meeting with clients or colleagues, praying, being with the people you love and care for, facing the situations or people you don't like, observing nature, playing with the dog – it all boils down to being more deeply connected. As you establish deeper connections, so your sense of significance will deepen as well.

One of the most profound sentences I have ever read was coined by Neale Donald Walsch when he said: 'In the absence of that which I am not, that which I am cannot exist.' This means that without the existence of everything outside of me, nothing inside of me can exist. It also relates to the African value of ubuntu, meaning 'I am because of you.' The 'you' can be personal or non-personal. The fact is that your existence is interdependent on the existence of everything else.

It is obvious that, in more simple language, we are talking about relationships. Thus, at any given moment one exists in relation to whatever and whoever else is present in the situation in which one finds oneself. For example, as I write this book, there is the relationship with myself, with the source of this information, with the chair I'm sitting on, with the pen I'm writing with and, to a certain extent, with you, the reader of the book. All of this gives rise to my current reality in this moment.

The relationships in which we find ourselves and to which we are connected in one way or another are the following.

The self

Arguably the most important relationship we will ever have is with ourselves.

If you believe it to be true that your inner world creates your outer world, you will know that the harder you work on developing, calming and enriching your inner world, the better your experience of the outer world will be. The self gives rise to the totality of all our perceptions and realities.

It is for this reason that we read self-help books, talk about self-mastery and engage in positive self-talk and selfdevelopment.

For the Buddha, life is all about the higher self where there is a connection with a self that is not plagued by the influences of the world and not driven by the ego – a self that would set us free from desire and from the discomfort of not having.

This relationship with the self dictates the quality of all other relationships we engage in. Our relationships with others often fail and our ability to be happy and at peace with ourselves is compromised when the relationship with the self is based on fear.

Bookstores and libraries are filled with books on the self. All the great psychologists, from Jung and Freud to Pavlov and Rogers, have dedicated great bodies of work to an analysis of the self. All religions emphasise the importance of the self because in your world you are the most important entity.

Without you, 'your world' cannot exist. Being at peace with the self and being in a good relationship with your world depend on the ability to focus on all three time frames the self operates on – the past, the present and the future.

Having said this, the present self should always remain at the centre. The reason for this is that the time zone that matters the most is the present and by dwelling too much in the past and the future you lose significance. For us to be at peace in the now and to have optimal relationships in the present, it is often necessary to go back to the past and heal the scars of yesterday – to make peace with what we've done wrong and the mistakes we've made. That healing will set us free to have a better relationship with the present. It is also important to spend time projecting the current self into the future to see what it is we still want to attain. That will give us insight into what actions we have to take now in the present to be able to meet the expectations we have of a future self.

Take time to spend with yourself, nurture your understanding of who you are and consolidate your core values and beliefs.

Set challenges to improve your mind, body and soul. Fall in love with who you are and begin the life-long journey of developing a positive and enriching relationship with yourself.

As with all relationships, this takes time, effort and a whole lot of work. Every moment is valuable because we are talking about you and you can only be of service and significance to yourself and others if you have a good relationship with the man/woman you see looking back at you in the mirror.

Nature and things

As I am writing this, it is midsummer and it's raining on the Highveld. An electrical storm with lightning and thunderbolts has just passed and I am becoming aware of and annoyed

by the leak in the roof that I've already had fixed twice this

summer.

No matter where you live, whether it is in the middle of a concrete jungle or in a rainforest, you will forever be in some relationship with nature. Due to our own planning and personal desires, we often stand in opposition to nature.

There is nothing that can spoil a picnic or a game of golf in the way a rainstorm or lightning can. We pray for rain because we need the crops to grow but, if it rains too often or for too long, we pray for the rain to stop so that we can harvest the

crops. In the context of meaning and significance, we need to exchange this combative relationship with nature for a much more peaceful one. We are not separate from nature; the only thing that separates us is our desire for things to be different so that nature will conveniently fit in with our arrangements.

This separation results in feelings of discomfort and negativity towards nature. As they say, 'go with the flow' and, instead of trying to impose your will on nature, rather become a part of it as nature is the mother who provides us with what we need to ensure our wellness.

You also have a relationship with 'things' – the furniture in your home, the painting against the wall, the ring on your finger, the car in your garage, the house you live in and many more. We know that these are our possessions and that we own them. This is a healthy situation until the tables are turned and the 'things' start owning us.

In the section 'You are what you have', we discussed how the mask of owning material things influences meaning. In our relationship with the things we own, we need to see these purely as enhancements of our lives and not allow them to become our lives. Achieving this relationship with things is essential to a peaceful state of mind. In a relationship where our significance is vested in what we own, we never feel content with what we have and constantly strive to acquire more and more. In this way, we become slaves to our possessions and that type of relationship leads only to a hollow and superficial type of happiness.

Animals

A recent documentary I watched on television revealed the relationship between guide dogs and blind people. It was impossible to watch that and not to feel the extremely deep bond between the owner and the dog. Our relationships with animals are among the most profound one can imagine. The domestic animal plays a huge part in the contentment and significance of the home. It teaches children how to care for what they love. These animals also serve as loyal companions and research has proven that while stroking an animal, your levels of stress decline and your feelings of wellness increase. In my own life I have watched our ginger cat show tremendous understanding of the state of mind my wife is in. After the death of her father, the cat would often gently pat my wife's face with his paw while gazing at her for long,

uninterrupted minutes.

Another group of animals consists of farm animals, some of which are bred purely for human consumption which, in most cases, is a little sickening because of man's need for meat.

This group also includes animals such as horses and camels that serve man and, when looked after correctly, can bring about good and meaningful relationships between man and

beast

Wild animals constitute the last group. Having grown up in Africa, we have the unique opportunity and privilege of still being able to see wild animals roaming around in their natural habitat. Again, this encourages a level of respect for these animals. The profound bond that can be forged between humans and wild animals has also been highlighted by research which shows that individuals who have difficulty in connecting with others as a result of disorders such as autism or retardation derive great benefit from swimming with dolphins, for example, or helping to take care of wild animals in captivity.

This, of course, must always be seen as a privilege. With all animals there is always the underlying negativity of abuse.

This wonderful, almost serene experience becomes void when people break the bond of respect and misuse their power over the animal kingdom in all forms of abuse.

As in nature, admiration and respect are essential to maintaining the relationship between ourselves and the

animal kingdom.

God

Whether you are a believer or not, you cannot deny that a great number of people have a relationship with God. For some it is a personal God and for some an impersonal God, but either way, meaning is derived from this relationship. Out of respect for the many and varied beliefs that people hold, I obviously don't want this section to be interpreted as being in any way dogmatic or religious.

Daily, billions of prayers are being offered up to God – some to ask, some to thank, some out of habit, some out of need, lots out of fear and a great deal, I hope, out of gratitude.

Whichever way you look at it, since time immemorial, people have generally had a need to connect in a relationship to something greater than themselves. This anchor is necessary in order to impart fulfilment to all relationships.

The relationship with God gives meaning to life as it transcends the ordinary and propels the mind and soul into

the extraordinary or mystical sphere.

At moments of true elation we need to believe that the feelings of wellbeing that accompany this emotion come from something greater than ourselves and, in our darkest hours, we want to feel that there is a power greater than human power in which we can trust. Whatever your beliefs, we know for a fact that this relationship with God or the divine or a higher force does create a sense of fulfilment and significance. The only harm that this relationship can do is when it abuses and is misdirected towards self-gain and the judgement of others. In its purest form it brings delight and contentment to those who choose to stand in this relationship.

People

This is where we stand or fall as Meaning Makers. None of the other relationships such as those with nature, things, animals, etc have the same profound effect on us as those we have with people. They can make us feel content and happy; they can make us experience disgust and hatred; we want to embrace them and we want to destroy them. They are our masters. They are here because we need them in order to grow and develop and they need us in the same way.

Martin Luther King Jnr said, 'In a real sense all life is interrelated.

All persons are caught in an inescapable network of mutuality, tied in a single garment of destiny. Whatever affects one directly affects all indirectly. I can never be what

I ought to be until you are what you ought to be and you can never be what you ought to be until I am what I ought to be.

This is the inter-related structure of reality.'

Relationships with people provide us with the perfect opportunity to practise the creation of meaning.

The elements we've discussed earlier such as self-expression, involvement, non-judgement, contribution and appreciation come alive when we apply them to our relationships with the intention of creating more meaning for ourselves and the people around us.

As we start going through the different types of relationships with people, keep the elements of creating meaning in mind and you will find that in some, these elements come naturally and you feel that you want to get involved and make a contribution while in others you will find it more difficult to express yourself and find real connections. In both instances the learning opportunities are vast. The key is to remain mindful of your intention to experience meaning and watch how these relationships challenge and reward you in asignificant way.

Following are a few of the possible types of relationships with people in which we find ourselves.

Parents and children

Definitely one of the most complicated relationships we will ever find ourselves in. During our childhood we are

impressionable and it is during this period that the people we spend most of our time with are our parents, hence the big influence they have on us in our earlier years. Most psychologists I know will have something to say about

the correlation between our behaviour as adults and the relationship we had with our parents while growing up.

Our earlier relationships with parents are involuntary and our self-expression is often formed and guided by their

principles and value systems. It is for this reason that we need to re-evaluate our beliefs, values and insights as we reach early adulthood. This is necessary in order to avoid remaining at the mercy of old beliefs that were ingrained in us by our parents and which are not serving us right now. I am sure you can think of a few yourselves and I am also sure you know that your parents did the best they could. This is no reason to reject your upbringing but merely to evaluate and differentiate between what is serving you in your life right now and what is not.

In later years the situation turns around, the young adults have their own children and a new cycle begins. It is here that insight becomes invaluable. There is arguably no greater responsibility than that of parenthood. Having insight into the impact that you as a parent can have on your children, especially during their early childhood, will go a long way towards ensuring that your influence on them will be a positive and healthy one. As Gibran says, be mindful at all times 'to be the bow that shoots the arrow and not to hold on to the arrow because of your own insecurity'. He also says that our children are not ours; they merely come though us.

We have often seen how parental abuse, disrespect and neglect perpetuate themselves over a number of generations.

Yes, this happens, but the cycle can be broken by you. You have the power to create a new value system, new positive beliefs, mutual respect, and a greater degree of significance and self-worth for yourself and your children.

Siblings and family

Within our families we also have the opportunity to interact with our siblings and extended family such as cousins,

uncles and aunts, and grandparents. This family context allows us to explore our self-expression and contribution to family members. It also helps us to understand boundaries.

For example, an older brother or sister might ask a younger one not to go into their room without permission or to stop bugging them.

In our relationships with siblings and other family members there is still fairly good parental guidance regarding respect and interaction which helps us understand how to relate to people. All of these relationships contribute in a very positive way to developing meaningful relationships within certain boundaries and guidelines. For example, my wife comes from a family of three children where she is the youngest and it is wonderful to observe the relationships she enjoys with her older brother and sister who always look out for her and want to protect her, and the levels of respect that exist between them.

I am completely aware that in all households there are many challenges, of which most can be overcome, but there can also be very deep-rooted problems such as abuse, disrespect and toxic relationships that can have tragic results. The focus here is on the healthy and functional relationships we have

with our family members.

Make no mistake, our family members also have the ability to push all the wrong buttons. This in itself is not a bad thing as it gives us the opportunity to find creative ways to deal with each other. Because they are related to us by blood, family members also often take liberties and so do we, but again, this gives us opportunities to explore better ways of managing our relationships.

Friends and acquaintances

In the book *Illusions*, Richard Bach says that your friends will know you better within the first minute of meeting you than your acquaintances will know you in a thousand years. Perhaps this is precisely the difference between acquaintances and friends. With the former there is some connection, a pleasant interaction and that is about it, while with latter there is a much deeper connection, an understanding of the essence of each other, a connection that goes deeper than time and space.

Many years ago, when a very good friend of mine left the country to settle in Germany, he gave me a book the subtitle of which stated that there is no such place as far away, and if you want to be with someone aren't you already there?

Testimony to the fact that separation in terms of time and space doesn't matter in real friendships because the bond between you goes beyond all of that.

With regard to acquaintances, one cannot downplay their importance. Of all the relationships you will have in life, the majority will be with acquaintances, hence the importance of creating and maintaining significance within these relationships. There is also the distinct possibility that when you maintain these relationships, some of them may develop into deeper friendships. It is important to note that even among acquaintances there is always the opportunity to create some meaningful experiences for both parties. In fact it is very easy to create that magical moment – be it a compliment, a hello or thank you, a smile, a word of advice, a hug or a cup of coffee. All these gestures at the right time and with the right intention have the potential to make a difference to the quality of your life and the lives of other people.

Under the category of acquaintances I also include those people you just happen to bump into in the course of daily living such as the security guard at the boom gate, the packer at the checkout till in the supermarket and the teller in the bank. These interactions have significance written all over

them.

In 2010, during the Soccer World Cup hosted by South Africa,

I asked a security guard whether he knew the score in the game that was currently being played. He told me, and it so happened that we rooted for different teams. Every time I go through that security checkpoint, and this man is on duty, he reminds me with a big smile that his team is doing much better than mine. Months later he told me that it is so nice to share a smile with me as most people just ignore him and see his interaction with them as nothing more than an annoyance.

Establishing significant interaction in this case was really as simple as asking for the score.

As for our friendships, to a great extent, they are the reason for our existence. There is nothing more valuable than connecting deeply with another human being, sharing a moment of greatness, looking at something together and sharing the same sense of wonder in the object or scene. It is in the context of these relationships that we get to be our true selves. We don't need to pretend or fear judgement as true friends accept us as we are including both our good and not-so-good points.

The more we understand the essence of meaning, the better friends we become. Through friendship there is the

opportunity to make a difference, to contribute to your friend's life and to show and experience appreciation. In my own life I treasure my friends as they allow me to be who I am. Over a period of time friendship builds up a history

and it is comforting to know that you have old friends who have known you through thick and thin, can bear witness to who you are and how you have grown and developed as a person, and that you can do the same for them. With these friends you can play the 'Do you remember?' game and reinforce your love and appreciation for one another over the years.

In the next topic we look at spouses and lovers. All of the wonderful characteristics of a great friendship can also be found in a loving spouse or life partner.

Spouses and life partners

Romantic love is a topic poets write about, singers sing about, writers write about, painters paint about, sculptors immortalise in stone, bronze or marble, and still there are not enough words, not enough expressions, not enough canvases and not enough paint to express this overwhelming emotion that cuts through everything. We read about it in religious writings and everybody who is anybody has sooner or later made a statement about love in some form. Neither young boys nor old men act their age when intoxicated by romantic love.

If you Google the words 'love' or 'romantic love' you find thousands and thousands of pages on the subject, too many to even try to consolidate into some sort of definition. Romantic love spans a whole spectrum of emotions, from raw sexual lust to a deep soul connection that exists outside the realm of words. There must be some truth in all of this as we all struggle to encapsulate the myriad feelings associated with love in

words.

Knowing how difficult it is to find the right words to express the emotions elicited by love, famous writers and poets often use imagery and paradox by way of illustration. Shakespeare did exactly that when he wrote, 'Love is a smoke made with the fume of sighs, being purged, a fire sparking in a lover's eyes. Being vexed, a sea nourished with lovers' tears, what is it else? A madness most discreet, a choking gall and a preserving sweet.' In the presence of such a master of words one almost feels completely incompetent to write on the elusive subject of love. Nevertheless it is a potent factor in romantic relationships and definitely the topic that gets the most attention on this planet.

Relationships between lovers provide a soul connection that gives flavour and colour to life. It becomes a reason

for existence and often the reason for giving up hope and becoming depressed when it doesn't work out the way we hoped it would.

In a meaningful, loving relationship there are values to uphold and the importance attributed to each one differs from person to person. Values such as trust, respect, communication, space, acceptance, honesty, commitment, appreciation, etc are all important to us and, when there is betrayal of even one of these values, the relationship is at risk of breakdown and eventual disintegration. It is then important to know that the significance of the relationship is built on these values.

To maintain significant relationships both partners should constantly maintain open communication about what is important to them and then agree to uphold the values they have agreed on.

To give an example, a good friend of mine got married but failed to have this default conversation with his wife prior to the marriage. For her, punctuality was important while he attributed very little value to it. Needless to say, he would agree to pick up the children from school at 14:00 and then only arrive at 14:30.

By that time the teacher would have called his wife who would be very upset. This became such an issue that a number of other values became linked to it such as disrespect, lack of trust and so forth. The marriage eventually disintegrated because of this.

Because you choose to live with someone you love and to share your living space, bathrooms, the remote, children and finances, it becomes necessary to have clarity on the values of each person, the roles they will fulfil and what is important to each person. Without this clarity it is easy to find yourself in a situation where the relationship has lost its significance and has become a burden to either one or both parties.

As you know, a loving and connected relationship has the potential to light up your life with meaning and significance or to destroy your passion and zest for life, leaving you in a dark and painful place with very little meaning. It is for these reasons that the choice of a life partner should be made with wisdom and insight.

Money

You must often have heard the saying, 'Money is the root of all evil.' The good news is that it is not. It is the love of money that is the root of all evil.

We all stand in some sort of relationship to money. For some it is like a good friend and the relationship is peaceful and mutually respectful. For others it is like facing an enemy – someone has to lose and someone will win. The reality is that whenever money becomes an opposing factor in your life it will remain an opponent that you'll face every month with the big showdown usually happening at the end of each month.

When it becomes an enabler that fulfils certain needs and allows you to operate in this world, money becomes a means towards an end. However, as with all things in life, when there is a relationship of fear it tends to polarise you and the relationship becomes toxic. When you live with the love of life rather than the love of money in your heart, the relationship becomes respectful and harmonious.

A realistic view of money is that it is a currency for energy. For a certain energetic output you will be rewarded in monetary terms. The problem begins when you consider the monetary reward to be too low for the work you put in. This is the time to reflect on what you do, who you work for, your expression of your talents and your self-worth, and then to re-evaluate your energy output in terms of the monetary reward you receive for it.

A last thought on money is to remember that it is an amplifier.

For example, if someone is negative, greedy, non-caring and disrespectful, money will amplify these qualities. The opposite is also true: money enhances the attributes of good heartedness and caring.

The objective is a harmonious balance between yourself, work and the value of money in your life.

It would be safe to say that the fundamental factor in all relationships, whether it is with the self, nature, animals, friends, lovers, family members or a God is based on love.

Love is the glue, the binding agent that keeps relationships afloat and that gives meaning to our interactions. In the absence of love there is no relationship. The intensity and type of love experienced may definitely vary between people, but its essence is always the same.

Finally, the sum total of our efforts to become Meaning Makers and to experience significance on this planet will,

in some way, always be a function of our ability to connect.

To connect to the self and to all that is outside the self, all of which and who, in reality, are there to assist the self in finding meaning.

As our consciousness evolves and as we become more 'awake' through seeking a deeper understanding, deeper experiencesand deeper relationships, we become better Meaning Makers. Through this process ofevolution we grow and so does our ability to manifest connected behaviour with everyone and everything in the universe.

A Stroke of Meaningfulness

Every time I have been truly unhappy in my life, it has had something to do with a relationship and not only with a romantic relationship. The unhappiness emanated from unsatisfactory relationships with people, myself, nature and many other aspects of life. Perhaps the lesson to be learned is that one cannot be in a discordant relationship with anything or anyone and still expect to be truly happy.

The Story of my Life

MEANING AND THE STORIES OF OUR LIVES

'There is no "this is the story of my life". Rather, "these are the stories of my life."'

Throughout this book you will find several short stories to explain a point or to give an example. This is done because nothing explains the meaning or the lack thereof in our lives better than a story.

In narrative psychology the method of healing and helping happens through asking questions so that the person on the couch can start telling his or her story. As soon as that happens the story can be dissected and show how meaning or the lack of meaning was construed.

A friend of mine, who is a narrative psychologist, once told me how a young lady suffering from anorexia and close to dying spoke about her life story day after day. She told him how she was rejected by her parents, how she never got attention from the boys in her class, how she stood in front of the mirror and all she could see was how ugly and fat she was. All of these events compounded in a profoundly nonliving relationship with herself. Furthermore, it isolated her as she was only involved in dieting and nothing else.

She started questioning her ability to add value to herself or her world and that propelled her into deeper depression. The downward spiral continued and it seemed clear that she was going to continue to diet until she died. Through the reconstruction of her life story Dr Roux succeeded in showing her that her perception gave rise to a false reality that was so warped that it was going to destroy her. He claims that by getting her to the point where she could understand her story she could heal herself and she did.

All of us are governed by a set of values, beliefs, experiences, etc that, when put together, give rise to a number of stories that form the central story of our lives. The good thing is that, because this is a story, at any given time we can push the pause button, relook the story, change the characters and head towards a different ending. You may feel that this is not possible for you, that there are just too many negatives in your life to be able to turn it around and begin to live a more meaningful life. Well, if you believe this and take it as truth, your perception will be your reality and that will be the story of your life.

There is another, much more significant option. You could take some personal time, as suggested in this book, and begin a journey back in time to unravel the beliefs that constrain you. You could test those stories that you live and which play over and over in your head, change the script and walk towards a new ending.

Here is a story that I lived and changed. I come from a family where the men are notoriously short-tempered and have fire in their bellies. My grandfather fought in a number of battles, held a high rank and commanded a number of men in times of war. My father grew up under his 'command' and is a dear man but also has a quick temper. Luckily, he has the ability to cool off as quickly as his temper flares up and to admit that he was wrong. He worked in the retail sector and had a number of staff under him who often remarked to my mother that they didn't know how she managed to live with him.

From a young age I also had a quick temper and didn't shy away from any type of confrontation. I married a soft-spoken, gentle wife and everyone warned her that I had a bad temper. Soon after we married, I had occasion to show my temper and, once I had reflected on my behaviour, I saw that this detracted from my relationship with her. By dissecting the story of the bad-tempered men in my family I vowed that this tendency would stop with me and started changing my life's story straight away. I became mindful of how I expressed myself and if, by dint of habit, I lost my temper I would immediately acknowledge my mistake and take action to prevent it. Today I can honestly say that although some of the men in my family are bad-tempered I am not one of them.

The meaning in our lives is construed by stories in our headsthat become our reality. Think of a good conversation with an old friend in which you tell him or her about your life and what happened during the years either before you met or during a period when you had no contact with each other.

What are you telling him/her? You are telling them a story with a plot and characters who play their roles in the story.

Now think about the stories you can tell an old friend about what made your life meaningful and those that made your life awful. The sum total of these is your life story. When we take the time to work through our life stories we get to the aha's about life and once we get to the aha's we can begin to change the story line.

These stories are so important to me that I am going to share a number of them with you. This will give you some insight into how meaning is constructed. The intention is also to add a practical section to the book where you can identify with the actual process of creating meaning.

While you read through them, reflect on all the aspects that contribute to meaning-making outlined in the pages of this book. I trust that in the stories that follow you will be able to identify fundamental elements that recur in the story of your own life.

The little boy and the blue balloon

In a play park one day a little boy was nagging his parents to buy him a bunch of balloons from the man who sold them in a multitude of colours at his stall.

'Dad, I love balloons and look, they are all in different colours,' he said. 'May I please have them?' His father finally relented and bought his son a bunch of balloons.

On their way out of the play park a little blue balloon said to the others, 'I am tired of being held down by a string.'

The big orange balloon replied, 'You shouldn't be tired because this is why you were made – to be blown up and held down by a string – and what is more, you should be glad that you have the opportunity to make a little boy happy.'

The yellow balloon overheard this conversations and said, 'Well, because we are filled with special air, all we want to do is go up, don't we? It makes us wonder what is up there.'

'Nothing,' said one of the older balloons. 'There is nothing but 0air up there.'

'But if there is air in us and air up there, that is just some more air,' argued the little blue balloon. 'Perhaps we will be freer when we are up there seeing that our essence is air.'

'No,' said the older balloon. 'The pressure changes us if we go too high. We will burst up there.'

Still the blue balloon was not satisfied. 'That's not such a bad thing,' he said, 'because then we will be one with the air and, seeing that we have air within us, all that we will be is ourselves.'

The yellow balloon interrupted by asking, 'But what will happen to our latex capsule?'

'Well, I guess it will fall back to earth and be destroyed but the good thing is that we won't need it,' said the little blue balloon.

'Stop talking nonsense,' said the grumpy old red balloon.

'How will you ever get the boy to let go of us? He is our owner now, remember.'

A moment passed and the little blue balloon said, 'Let's ask him!'

'And how will we do that?' the silver balloon asked as all the balloons were becoming kind of excited about this idea of going up into the sky and becoming one with who they already were rather than separate in their colourful latex capsules filled with a little bit of special air, confined to a string.

'Well,' said the little blue balloon, 'we are in the boy's hand and his hand is linked to his arm and his arm to his shoulder and his shoulder to his neck and his neck to his head and his head has ears on it, so we will just send him a message through our strings and, if it is true that we all are one, he should get the message, right?'

'Okay,' said the red balloon. 'Let's go ahead and let's send that message, you guys.'

A millisecond later the little boy looked up at the balloons, opened his hand and let them go.

His dad tried to grab them but they were gone. He looked at the child and said, 'Why did you do that?'

The little boy smiled and said, 'Because they asked me to.'

Preparing a leg of lamb

Many years ago someone told me this story about a Greek family who loved to cook a leg of lamb on a Sunday afternoon.

Every Sunday, before the wife started cooking the meat, she would ask her husband to remove the last 5 cm of the shinbone. One Sunday, while he was carrying out this task, he asked his wife why it was that every Sunday she asked him to cut off this bit of the shinbone. She replied that this was the way her father and mother had cooked it ever since she could remember and that this was the right way of preparing the roast.

The man decided to call his mother-in-law right away to find out why this became a custom in her family, whether this influences the taste of the meat and whether they perhaps used the part of the shinbone that had been cut off for some other purpose. She replied that she really had no idea why they had been doing this, but that this was the way her mother had always prepared the roast when she was a child. She added that the grandmother was right there and she would hand her the phone so that she could explain why this was the custom in the family.

The grandmother took the phone and the son-in-law explained to her how he cuts off the end of the shinbone every Sunday, as his wife's parents had also done while she was growing up, and that he was wondering what the reason for this was. The grandmother hesitated for a moment before asking, 'Do you do this every Sunday when you cook lamb?' The son-in-law confirmed that this same custom that prevailed in his in-laws' home was observed in his family's home. Very confused, the grandmother told him that she had no idea why he goes to the trouble to do this. The only reason she and her husband used to do this was because they had a very small roasting pan and it was not possible to fit the leg of lamb into it without first removing part of the shinbone.

So, it was only in the third generation that someone became curious enough about a family's traditional way of doing something to question the reason for its existence and it took two generations for this to be changed.

The question is: What perception, habit or belief is there in your life that might be holding you back? You can change these if you are curious enough to ask the right questions and to challenge the traditional way of doing things.

The fear virus I contracted at birth

I was born to a mother and father who had difficulty in conceiving a child and, after thirteen years of marriage, I went to a picnic with my dad and came home with my mom.

Nine months later, I came to the planet and I've been here for the past forty-seven years. After waiting thirteen years for a child, my parents were naturally very protective over me and of course there is nothing wrong with that.

My mother (whom I love dearly) is a woman who is mostly governed by fear. She is one of those caring people who want everything to go well and want this so badly that they live with the constant fear that something will go wrong. I contracted this fear virus from her at birth. I remember times when my dad didn't arrive home from work exactly when she expected him to and on those occasions she would sit me down to wait for him. Those minutes – sometimes stretching into an hour – were filled with fear. She would often be so fearful that something had happened to him that she would phone the hospital or a friend to express her worry.

At age seventy-nine things haven't changed for my mother as her own health and that of my dad, who is eighty-five, is now declining. The fear of illness and the unknown is now even more prevalent in her life than ever. So now you know that I grew up with fear as my twin brother. Needless to say, it didn't take long for fear to start ruling my life. I became fearful of illness, of not being good enough at what I do, of not having enough money, and the list goes on and on.

The fear grew to the point that, from time to time, it paralysed me to such an extent that I literally could do nothing but worry. By now you are hoping that I will be able to tell you how, as a conscious individual such as myself, who spends his life researching, teaching and writing books, has learned how to overcome fear. Sorry, but I can't. I still fight this battle with fear daily and most days I win. Yes, sometimes even a few months go by during which I feel that I have triumphed over my fear, but every now and then my dark twin brother returns to remind me of how fearful I am. I then practise the skills I've acquired to move away from it and, as I've said, I succeed more often than not. Let me say that I believe we choose our parents because we need to learn what we came to earth to learn and I have chosen my mother so that I can overcome fear.

My challenge is to look at this page in the storybook of my life and ask myself (which I often do) how I can disempower this debilitating belief.

There may be a page in your book that is similar to mine, or perhaps you suffered abuse, neglect, shame or grief while growing up. The secret is to discover the link between early experience and those disempowering self-beliefs you hold as an adult that are holding you back from realising your

potential. Only then can you move forward in a positive and significant way.

The old man with the wise words

During my childhood I mostly felt that I didn't fit in anywhere.

It was as if my internal dialogue was telling me that no one understood or wanted to understand how I felt. Whenever I tried to express myself all I got in return from most people was a vacant stare as if to say 'What are you on about?'

Later, a good friend from school went off to do his compulsory military training and asked me to occasionally drop in at his dad's home just to see if the old man was okay. These visits became more frequent as I started to speak to Uncle Danie about life and, in some wonderful way, we connected. He was always in his dirty working clothes, with rough hands and an unshaven beard. When I'd arrive at his home, he'd stop whatever he was busy with and invite me in for a cup of tea.

The teapot was usually already on the stove brewing and the tea that came from that pot was so strong that you had to add loads of milk and sugar to it to make it palatable.

At these times he would ask me what was on my mind. At age sixteen it was mostly girls and then, of course, my early search for meaning. During one of these visits I had a heavy heart. I'd made a mistake, had done something I wasn't proud of, and wanted to know how to handle this. The first part of Uncle Danie's advice was to go and make peace with the person concerned and ask for forgiveness, which I did. I had been beating myself up for allowing this to happen and had felt as if I'd lost my way. He took me outside, picked up a metal bar, put it on the paving and then used a bottle of spray paint to spray a silver line on it. He removed the metal bar and said to me, 'If this silver line is the line of a good life, I can tell you now that you won't be able to stay on it one hundred percent of the time in your life, but the secret is to always return to it. When you stray from the line, make sure that your head and heart always point towards it so that you can find your way back.'

I learned that day that we all make mistakes and disappoint ourselves and others, but what is important in life is to always have a moral compass that indicates the way back to a good and upright life.

Divided in religion and united in faith

In the Dutch Reformed Church the procedure is simple and sombre. You go in, you sit, you listen, you sing three hymns and you leave. No funny business. You are in at 09:00 and out at 09:45 and God forbid that the Reverend should keep you there till 10:00. At the next church meeting you can bet that some of the elders will bring it to the Reverend's attention that his service ran 15 minutes late last time. Well, I can't speak for services these days, but it was like that while I was still attending.

During my second year at university I dated a girl who was not a member of my church. She and her family attended a charismatic church. My visits to their home went well except for the Sunday morning service. We went into church at 09:00 and came out at 11:30. We sang more in those two and a half hours than we did in a year at my church. Needless to say I was petrified of the pastor who was not on a pulpit but on a stage, and who wasn't 'preaching' but 'screaming' at us.

This was my first time in a charismatic church and I wasn't prepared for the difference in approach at all.

Back at my hostel that evening I called the only person who I knew could help me find context and insight into my very disturbing mindset. André is most probably the one person on this planet who has given me more insight into life than everybody else I know combined. In his usual calm and passive way he listened and said that I should come and visit him in Johannesburg the following weekend. I wanted some answers and kept on nagging, but he all he did was insist that I visit him.

The next Saturday I arrived at his home in Johannesburg where we spent time with friends and didn't talk about my confusion regarding the church, God and different faiths.

On the Sunday morning we got up early and went for a drive. André stopped at a number of churches, synagogues, mosques and temples, and asked me to just sit there and feel the energy. We spent a great deal of time driving around from one venue to the other. Later, at lunch, he asked me what was different about all of these places of worship and I could come up with quite a few differences. He then asked me what I thought was the one thing that was the same. In this way I got to figure out for myself that when it comes to the important things in life, it is easy to get trapped in all that is different, and it's therefore much better to focus on what we have in common.

Follow your bliss – at any cost

While I was lecturing at a university I once attended a conference held in a posh conference centre in Midrand. As I sat listening to speaker after speaker, hearing their different views, taking notes and evaluating what they said, I actually felt a little disappointed with the quality of the conference and the speakers who had been hired.

Then the master of ceremonies announced a speaker from Canada, a man by the name of Bill Gibson. As a well qualified academic I wasn't sure that I could learn much from a Canadian business speaker. However, I was taken aback when he got on stage, took his jacket off and threw it into the crowd. In the first few seconds he had the crowd clapping and laughing and that intrigued me. A few minutes later I thought, typical North American style, all huff and puff and no substance. Yet, as he proceeded to effortlessly switch between humour and context, I was proven wrong. In fact he was the one speaker who gave me the most value to take away from the conference.

After his speech I walked up to him and introduced myself and, on my feedback form, requested him to please contact me. He later did so and, to cut a long story short, we became very close friends.

I was still lecturing and every now and then we would meet up for a coffee or a bite to eat, and each time I learned more from him. On one of these occasions I expressed my frustration with lecturing and running a small consultancy business on the side. He then asked me the most powerful question anyone can ask another: 'What will give the most meaning to your life, Rinus?' I didn't even have to think about the answer. That December I left the university to follow my bliss, to do what I really, really love, to create significance in my life and to become the master of my own destiny. Yes, I have had hard times and yes, I sometimes hankered after that predictable pay cheque at the end of each month, but did I ever regret my decision? Never.

What it is that really turns you on? If you know this, you are eighty percent of the way there in the process of creating meaning.

The world is changing. For too long people have gotten away with doing an average job while being paid an above average salary. No longer can people retire at sixty-five and live on the proceeds of what they've achieved during their working lives for the rest of their days.

In view of these radical shifts in the world of work it is now more necessary than ever to find your bliss and to do it with passion and enthusiasm. If you're able to do that, why should you ever want to retire?

Create the creative spirit

There is a certain spirit one has when young – a spirit of can do! At that stage one lives as if everything is possible and one is willing to grab life and wrestle with it until everything goes one's way and all is fixed and fine. Sometimes, as we grow older, we become a bit more cynical, a bit less creative, believe less in miracles and give up a little on our dreams.

There were times in the hostel room at university when my friends and I had all the answers that the world needed. In theory we could fix any problem the country had and make a difference in an instant. During those days in that room the creative juices were flowing and the debates were fierce but

all focused on finding solutions and a better way. We were not afraid to share our dreams and were all most definitely going to live magnificent and meaningful lives.

Late at night and in the early mornings my friend Anton and

I sat and discussed everything that would make our lives significant and fabulous. Today we still see each other and talk a little about the weather and little about work and not a lot about our dreams.

Not too long ago we had another great conversation about life. At that moment it was almost as if we had found our fire again and the passion was heavy in our chests. The key to a meaningful life is to keep the creative spirit active and alive.

Someone once said that when you lose your dreams, you die.

Get together with people who have a positive and possibility orientated mindset. Start sharing your dreams with one another. Connection is key in the process of creativity and the more you talk about possibilities, the more possible they become.

Death and significance

On Sundays my late father-in-law and I used to have a long conversation which usually revolved around a state of mind that appeared on Sundays at about 4:00 pm and would leave again at about 7.00 pm. Both of us suffered from 'Sunday blues' and our regular Sunday conversations would be devoted to how to handle and beat these blues.

At eighty-five he became weaker and one could somehow see that his time here was running out. On my wife's return from a visit to her father, she delivered a message to me from him – he asked if I could please come and see him and that I bring pen and paper with me so that I could write down a few important things.

On a Monday morning my sister-in-law and I arrived at the old-age home where he was staying. Not long after that he asked to speak to me in private. He asked me if I'd brought the pen and paper which I took out to start writing. He said that at his funeral he would like me to say a few words and thank a few people. He gave me a short list and, after he was finished, I asked him why he didn't mention his three children and whether I could thank them too. He replied that I must please not do that. I was stunned as I knew how much he loved them. When I asked why not he said, 'I'm afraid I could say something that would make the one feel less important

than the other and then they would, for the rest of their lives, wonder whether I had loved them equally.' He said he often told them what they meant to him and it would be enough to leave it at that. Remarkable sensitivity, I thought.

He also made me promise that in my eulogy, I would not make a fuss about him and not say anything about him that would give stature to his life. He said that he had lived a good life and wanted to die a humble man. I told him I would not say anything untrue about him and he made me promise to stick only to the thank-you list and leave it at that. I promised and said goodbye. Two weeks later he died. At his funeral I saw why it was not necessary to say anything more. He had lived a life without ego and in that egoless space his spirit had blossomed.

Your English is useless

When you hear from an early age that you cannot do something, the chances are that, as you get older, you will believe it and it will become a truth in your life. Having grown up in an Afrikaans home with parents who were not fluent in English, I somehow always had the notion that I was not good at languages – hence my inability to speak and write correctly in English.

How I struggled with the language and some of mistakes I made in my school essays are still the butt of family jokes.

I distinctly remember how a high school teacher wrote on my report card that I would never have a general command of the English language. He even went so far as to call my

parents in to tell them how poor my command of the English language was.

Then, in grade eleven, I met an English girl and we started seeing each other. Her parents couldn't speak a word of Afrikaans and she had a very limited ability to understand my

language. Between the two of us we had to make some plan to communicate. At first it was an absolute joke although we both really struggled to communicate meaningfully. As time passed we broke up but stayed friends and kept encouraging each other to learn the second language in an environment where neither of us was afraid to make mistakes and express ourselves. In this way we both gained confidence and my English became better and better.

My parents were amazed at my new-found ability to speak the language and converse in it. Although they still often tell the story of how bad my essays were, today they say that I can be proud of having written and published seven books. As for me, I had the urge to send my high school English teacher a copy of my first book with a nasty note attached, but I resisted it.

The same applies to a person's ability to do mathematics. Yes, you have a certain aptitude for certain subjects, but the two biggest reasons why students struggle with maths is firstly when they hear from their parents that no one in the family has ever been any good at maths, and secondly most maths teachers don't know how to build self-esteem in students who believe they cannot master maths.

Again we see that meaning is created through creativity, willingness and a firm belief in possibility.

The great walk amongst us

It's another day of one-to-one conversations with individuals in the Vaal Triangle at a chemical plant. The objective is to talk about how meaningful the individual's life is and to discuss ways of creating a meaningful personal and work life.

A tall dark man with a short-sleeved checked shirt walks into the office. He introduces himself and takes a seat. He is a very unassuming man with a calm demeanour. We talk about his background and how he is doing within the new structure of the company. The conversation gently winds down and progresses into what it takes to live a significant life. He tells me that he learned a long time ago that what matters is not what happens to you, but rather what you do with what happens to you.

He tells me that his wife had a brain tumour removed which left her a different woman from the person he married years ago. I take the opportunity to ask him how he is coping with such a dramatic change in his personal life. He smiles and says they are working through it, that he learned such a lot about himself as a result and that it brought their family much closer to each other. I express how I appreciate people who can come through adversity and remain so positive about life.

He continues to talk and tells me how his family was held up at gunpoint by robbers one night, and how one of the robbers punched his wife in the face and kicked his youngest son when he tried to take care of his injured mother. He says that the burglars continuously called them white trash as they beat them up.

'How did you handle it?' I ask. He tells me the rest of the story of how the night played out and how the family survived.

Amazingly, he tells me how he kept thinking about what must have gone wrong in the young robbers' lives for them to have acted the way they did and why they saw the family as 'white trash'.

He personally went on an inward and outward journey to make peace with what happened and with himself. He

organised a choir competition at his church and explained the reconciliation that took place when people of all races participated and shared their views.

While he is sharing these stories with me and how he made peace with himself and the world, I can't hold back my tears. I just look at this ordinary man with an extra-ordinary mindset.

He works in the finance department of his company, has put three children through university, has gone through so much hardship and yet he is beaming with a positive light. Who would have thought that I would meet a Master of Life at a chemical plant in the Vaal Triangle?

I am now more sure than ever that the great don't have a special place where they hang out – they walk amongst us!

The meaningful mentor

I can count on one hand the people who stepped up and mentored me in my life but one thing is for certain – the value they added cannot be gained by studies or experience. In my third year at university the marketing manager of Toyota came to the campus to address the students. He was softspoken, had a calmness about him and was professionally dressed. By the end of the hour-long presentation I knew that

I wanted this man to mentor me.

Twenty-seven years later I still have a relationship with Brand Pretorius. He retired as CEO of McCarthy's in 2011 and is still active in the business world, but when I send him an sms or leave a message for him to call me, he responds as soon as possible.

The most important thing I have learned from Brand has very little to do with business principles or how a company should be run. Instead I have learned that there is nothing more important in life than the connections you establish while interacting with people. When Brand interacts with you, you are the focus of his attention. He makes you feel as if you are the most important person in his life at that moment and chances are that in fact that you are. Beyond all this lies the willingness to give time and energy to someone who has the potential to develop.

If you think about mentorship and the process of creating meaning you will find that it is a very rewarding activity.

You get to express your knowledge and wisdom, you get involved in the life of someone who needs you, and you make a contribution and feel appreciated. All of these elements contribute to meaningful interactions. We need more people like Mr Pretorius who are willing to give unconditionally of their time and ability to help and watch others grow.

The key is to look around you. I am sure that there are a number of people who would love to be mentored by someone like you – someone who is serious about creating meaning. When you reach out and give of your time, energy and ability to the mentee, you are not only creating meaning for yourself and the mentee, but also fostering behaviour that will change the course of your future and ensure a world where possibilities exist for more than just a few people.

END... ?

THE END ... CORRECTION, THERE IS NO END

'Within the end lingers the promise of a new beginning.'

The end ...
correction, there is no end

In our world of duality, for every beginning there must be an end and so I've come to the end of this book. The book may well end here, but the journey ... well, the journey never ends.

When you put the book away your lungs will be filled with another breath and a new thought will enter your mind only to leave it again when you exhale, and so the process will continue.

Being meaningful is not an event but a journey and some days will be more meaningful to you than others. Then there will be the days when you will feel empty and meaningless, yet when you reflect, you may find that those 'meaningless' days contributed in a wonderful way to your personal growth. The main thing is to be thankful for both the good days and the not-so-good days.

In every moment of every day lies the opportunity to discover meaning. The more we grow and

the more we are awake, the better the chances for us to find meaning in every moment. When you breathe out for the last time, another journey awaits you, one that we may explore in another book at another time.

My final words are that this is your life. Whether you believe you will come back again, or that when you die the lights go off and that is it, or that beyond this life there is another life, is kind of irrelevant right now because this is the life you have for now. You came here with a blank canvas and you leave here with a picture. My question to you is: Are you enjoying the painting you are creating? I hope so. I hope that wherever you may find yourself at this moment, whether you are elated with happiness or sick with sadness, you will know that everything you experience could be meaningful and significant in terms of your growth. Whatever your picture

looks like, you can turn it all around to your advantage and experience your essence which is pure love.

All our fear, pain, darkness, unhappiness and discontent have their source in ignorance.

When we choose to seek meaning and live it incrementally as we find it, we become less ignorant and more connected. Finally we find that in every ending lies the promise of a new and meaningful beginning.

… And, at the end of it all, everything will cease to exist and nothing will remain … until something is created.

9 780620 526616